Praying the Scriptures

Litanies for Sunday Worship

JEREMIAH D. WILLIAMSON

Church
NEW YORK

Unless otherwise noted, the Scripture quotations contained herein are from
the New Revised Standard Version Bible, copyright © 1989 by the Division of
Christian Education of the National Council of Churches of Christ in the U.S.A.
Used by permission. All rights reserved.

Cover design by Laurie Klein Westhafer
Typeset by Linda Brooks

A catalog record of this book is available from the Library of Congress.

ISBN-13: 978-0-89869-920-3 (pbk.)
ISBN-13: 978-0-89869-921-0 (ebook)

Church Publishing, Incorporated.
19 East 34th Street
New York, New York 10016

www.churchpublishing.org

To my biggest fans:
Oscar, Isaiah, and, especially, Jennifer

And to the people who pray with me:
St. Andrew's Episcopal Church, Toledo, Ohio

CONTENTS

Open my lips, O Lord,
And my mouth shall proclaim your praise.

Prayer is both one of the simplest and most daunting tasks of the Christian life. It can be as simple as "thank you" or "help!" and yet even Jesus' own disciples, those who heard Jesus' own prayers, still asked him for instruction.

As a parish priest, I am frequently asked for guidance in learning to pray. Like the first disciples, we're still asking for help. And, of course, when asked, I can share a variety of methods and techniques; I can offer examples. There are many forms of prayer but I have found, and perhaps you have as well, that not every form works for me. I should say I'm sure they work; I suspect God hears even our clumsiest prayers; I am confident God appreciates the time and effort of our honest attempts. But not every style of prayer speaks in my language.

For me, it is writing; writing is my prayer language. I did not really discover to what extent writing prayers would become my language for prayer until I started writing them for my congregation. You are holding my prayers—my offerings to God, to my parish, and now my offering to you and to your church. I discovered quickly that these prayers were *my* prayers only for a short time. As soon as they are prayed within communal worship, they become the prayers of the people. These prayers, these forms, take on new life as they carry your concerns, cradle your thanksgivings, and join the prayers of your heart.

The prayers in this book are shaped by the Holy Scriptures. I found my voice in the ancient voices of the biblical authors. As in the Anglican Prayer Book tradition, biblical language is the foundation of each and every collection of prayers. Using the texts given each week in the Revised Common Lectionary, I wrote prayers that, I hope, speak to the issues of our world in the familiar language and images of our sacred texts.

By doing so, my intention was to create a more cohesive liturgical experience. In the context of thoughtful worship planning, the prayers, scripture readings, sermon, and hymnody should all speak to the same themes; they should reinforce and enhance each other. My hope is that each week the concerns of the world are filtered anew through the sacred text and the rhythm of the Church.

I first started writing these prayers because I noticed in my own parish, and in other parishes where I have served and worshiped, that the time of congregational intercessions had little energy. We were rotating a few of the six forms found in the 1979 Book of Common Prayer and had been for decades. They are lovely forms, poetic and comprehensive, but there was just no energy. I could watch folks in the pews zone out and not because they did not value that time of prayer together. They value the opportunity very much. However, it was one of the few places in the Sunday service that was not being approached creatively or thoughtfully. And so I started writing prayers that would engage the congregation, prayers that would feel fresh and connected.

It is my hope that this collection incites prayer in your congregation and in your life. Whether these are prayed communally or in private devotions, I hope that they help you find your own prayer language. I believe every prayer is a poem—words strung together between the human heart and the heart of God. And so with that, let us pray.

ABOUT THIS BOOK

Each litany is essentially structured to adhere to the form suggested in the Book of Common Prayer. That means each Sunday, while praying the prayers, the congregation will pray for: the Church, the nation and the world, the created order, the local community, those who suffer, and the departed. Intercessors may choose to add additional petitions when a need arises.

It is perfectly appropriate to use the following prayers in your Sunday worship as written. You may, however, adapt them for your local community. The intercessor who leads the congregation in prayer might, for example, name the city, town, or village where the church is located. When members of the congregation die, they should be named within the people's prayers.

I have included some rubrics in the text for the intercessor. While I have directed a moment of silence after each petition, some congregations might choose to instead pray aloud in those places. I direct the intercessor to invite thanksgivings and petitions during the prayers; this practice may or may not work in your congregation.

I prefer the congregation and the Intercessor to share the prayers. Each litany has a call and response. This call and response is repetitive. I chose this style for two reasons: First, I don't want the congregation tied to the script. I want the prayers to develop a rhythm, to feel organic. At my parish, we print only the call and response. The petitions are printed only for the Intercessor.

It is Episcopal tradition for the presider to add a concluding collect to the end of the prayers. I have included some in this book. Worship books from other traditions offer additional options.

Finally, because the prayers are based on the Sunday lectionary, they can also be used in private devotions as a way of meditating on Sunday scriptures.

YEAR A

People of God, come, let us walk in the light of the Lord. Let us pray to the Lord, saying, "Teach us your ways, O God, *that we may walk in your paths.*"

Wake from sleep, O God, your Church. Let us lay aside the works of darkness and put on the armor of light. Let us live honorably as salvation draws ever nearer.
Silence
Teach us your ways, O God,
That we may walk in your paths.

Wake from sleep, O God, this nation. May we beat our swords into plowshares, and our spears into pruning hooks. May we learn war no more.
Silence
Teach us your ways, O God,
That we may walk in your paths.

Wake from sleep, O God, your creation. May the mountains rise to meet you and the crops of the fields burst forth in praise.
Silence
Teach us your ways, O God,
That we may walk in your paths.

Wake from sleep, O God, this city. May there be peace and prosperity within our walls. Make clear our paths that we may walk in your light.
Silence
Teach us your ways, O God,
That we may walk in your paths.

Wake from sleep, O God, those in pain and sadness. Deliver them from their darkness that they may rejoice in your light. May all those waiting for healing find your salvation is near.
Invite the congregation to add their petitions and thanksgivings, followed by silence
Teach us your ways, O God,
That we may walk in your paths.

Wake all your people from sleep, O God. Prepare your saints for that day when the Son of Man will return, with the saints at rest, to reign with us forever and ever.
Silence
Teach us your ways, O God,
That we may walk in your paths.

Friends, may the God of hope fill you with all joy and peace in believing. Let us come before the Lord, praying, *"Blessed are you, Lord God; may the earth be filled with your glory."*

Grant your Church, O God of encouragement, to live in harmony with one another, in accordance with Christ Jesus, so that we may glorify you with one voice. Make us a people of repentance and bless us with your Holy Spirit and fire.
Silence
Blessed are you, Lord God;
May the earth be filled with your glory.

Grant this nation, O God of justice, the will to defend the needy and the poor. May we sincerely work for that day when hurt and destruction are no more.
Silence
Blessed are you, Lord God;
May the earth be filled with your glory.

Grant your creation, O God of faithfulness, the hope of renewal. May we who are stewards of this earth, also live at peace with all you have created.
Silence
Blessed are you, Lord God;
May the earth be filled with your glory.

Grant this city, O God of understanding, prosperity. May all people know and do justice. Teach us and our leaders how best to meet the needs of all our neighbors.
Silence
Blessed are you, Lord God;
May all the earth be filled with your glory.

Grant all the needy, O God of steadfast love, your mercy. Prove yourself to be a God of righteousness and faithfulness. To all their pain and suffering bring your healing and peace. With your winnowing fork clear from their lives all the forces of oppression.
Invite the congregation to add their petitions and thanksgivings, followed by silence
Blessed are you, Lord God;
May all the earth be filled with your glory.

Grant to those who have died, O God of hope, eternal life in you. Bring the departed into your glorious dwelling where all their hope will be fulfilled in your Christ.
Silence
Blessed are you, Lord God;
May all the earth be filled with your glory.

Sisters and brothers, strengthen your hearts, for the coming of the Lord is near. Let us seek the Lord, praying, "Let us see your glory, O Lord; *come to us and save us!"*

Lord, save your Church from weakness of heart. Give us strength to prepare this world for the coming of your Christ and give us patience when it seems Christ's kingdom does not come quickly enough.
Silence
Let us see your glory, O Lord;
Come to us and save us!

Lord, save this nation from disordered priorities and misplaced hope. May our values mirror your values. May we be a nation that offers justice to the oppressed, food to the hungry and care to the stranger.
Silence
Let us see your glory, O Lord;
Come to us and save us!

Lord, save your creation from human misuse. Bless us to play a part in the redemption you have planned for all of creation.
Silence
Let us see your glory, O Lord;
Come to us and save us!

Lord, save this city from hopelessness. Give us a vision and a future. Raise up prophets who will speak hope and encouragement to the people of our region.
Silence
Let us see your glory, O Lord;
Come to us and save us!

Lord, save the sick and the sorrowful in the midst of their affliction. May they experience the healing work of their Messiah. Make happy all those who have you for their help.
Invite the congregation to add their petitions and thanksgivings, followed by silence
Let us see your glory, O Lord;
Come to us and save us!

Lord, bless all members of your heavenly kingdom. May they obtain eternal joy and gladness in your presence—where sorrow and sighing are no more.
Silence
Let us see your glory, O Lord;
Come to us and save us!

Grace to you and peace from God our Father and the Lord Jesus Christ. Let us appeal to the Lord, praying, "Restore us, O God of hosts; *show the light of your countenance and we shall be saved."*

We ask you, O God, to bless your Church. Give us your grace. Stir up your strength and come to help us even as we declare the gospel concerning your Son.
Silence
Restore us, O God of hosts;
Show the light of your countenance and we shall be saved.

We ask you, O God, to bless this nation. May our leaders not trust in their own strength but in you, O God of hosts. Teach us to refuse the evil and choose the good.
Silence
Restore us, O God of hosts;
Show the light of your countenance and we shall be saved.

We ask you, O God, to bless this planet. By your creative power bring forth new life in the places in which we have reaped too much or sown too little.
Silence
Restore us, O God of hosts;
Show the light of your countenance and we shall be saved.

We ask you, O God, to bless our city. Let your hand be upon us. Guide and strengthen all those who find themselves in difficult situations—especially young and single parents.
Silence
Restore us, O God of hosts;
Show the light of your countenance and we shall be saved.

We ask you, O God, to bless all those who are distressed. Hear their prayers, O Shepherd of the flock. May they take comfort in the knowledge that you are with them.
Invite the congregation to add their petitions and thanksgivings, followed by silence
Restore us, O God of hosts;
Show the light of your countenance and we shall be saved.

We ask you, O God, to bless all who have died. Welcome into your heavenly kingdom all who are called to be saints.
Silence
Restore us, O God of hosts;
Show the light of your countenance and we shall be saved.

Come let us adore Christ, the Lord. Let us pray, "Glorious Lord, *grant us your peace.*"

Christ the Lord, we humbly adore you: make joyful our hearts. Strengthen your Church with humility and faith that we might triumph over the power of evil.
Silence
Glorious Lord,
Grant us your peace.

Christ the Lord, we humbly adore you: you abhor neither the simple nor the lowly. Shine your light on all the world that the nations may look upon your truth and find their salvation.
Silence
Glorious Lord,
Grant us your peace.

Christ the Lord, we humbly adore you: may all of creation burst forth in songs of praise. May all the works of your hand glorify you.
Invite the congregation to add their thanksgivings, followed by silence
Glorious Lord,
Grant us your peace.

Christ the Lord, we humbly adore you: summon the people of the city to yourself. May all of the distractions and heartache of our lives fade away in the joy of your presence.
Silence
Glorious Lord,
Grant us your peace.

Christ the Lord, we humbly adore you: you love us so dearly. Grant your healing grace to sinners, to the poor, to those in need of love. Open your arms to the sick and the lonely.
Invite the congregation to add their petitions, followed by silence
Glorious Lord,
Grant us your peace.

Christ the Lord, we humbly adore you: all glory be given to you. You blessed our earthly bodies with your birth; and you promise to raise us to new life by your death and resurrection.
Silence
Glorious Lord,
Grant us your peace.

Christmas 1

The Word became flesh and lived among us, and we have seen his glory, the glory as of a father's only son, full of grace and truth. We are witnesses, praying, "Shine forth in our lives, O Lord. *Hallelujah!*"

Abba, Father, you have received us as your children. Make our hearts shine ever brighter with the pure light of Christ, that all people might witness your all-encompassing love.
Silence
Shine forth in our lives, O Lord.
Hallelujah!

Almighty God, let all the nations witness your glory. Cause righteousness and praise to cover the earth.
Silence
Shine forth in our lives, O Lord.
Hallelujah!

Great Lord, you are mighty in power: you graciously make the earth to burst forth with green plants; you provide food for flocks and herds; you give us the resources to thrive on this planet. May we be thankful in our hearts and generous in our lives.
Invite the congregation to add their thanksgivings, followed by silence
Shine forth in our lives, O Lord.
Hallelujah!

O God, it is you who establishes peace. Comfort your people with safety and security; assure us that it is not by our own strength, but by your goodness, that we can rest in quiet confidence.
Silence
Shine forth in our lives, O Lord.
Hallelujah!

Loving God, you are the healer of the brokenhearted; it is you who binds up their wounds; you lift up the lowly. Clothe your children with the garments of health and salvation.
Invite the congregation to add their petitions, followed by silence
Shine forth in our lives, O Lord.
Hallelujah!

O God, you sent your Son to redeem us from sin and death: draw us closer to your Son Jesus—into your heart, both now and in the life to come.
Silence
Shine forth in our lives, O Lord.
Hallelujah!

Sisters and brothers, let the same mind be in you that was in Christ Jesus. With humble hearts let us say to the Lord, "Lord Jesus, *we bow our hearts at your name.*"

Jesus, we exalt your name in all the world! Bless your Church. Inspire us by the Holy Spirit to confess you as Lord over all we are, all we do and all we hope to do.
Silence
Lord Jesus,
We bow our hearts at your name.

Jesus, we exalt your name in all the world! Bless the people of the world. May the whole world experience your peace.
Silence
Lord Jesus,
We bow our hearts at your name.

Jesus, we exalt your name in all the world! Bless our planet. Make us faithful stewards of all the works of your fingers. Forgive us when we fail to respect your creatures: the beasts of the field, the birds of the air, and the fish of the sea.
Silence
Lord Jesus,
We bow our hearts at your name.

Jesus, we exalt your name in all the world! Bless our city and our region. Give us renewed hope and purpose as we begin this new year.
Silence
Lord Jesus,
We bow our hearts at your name.

Jesus, we exalt your name in all the world! Bless the sick and the lonely and all those in great need. Make your face to shine on them and be gracious to them.
Invite the congregation to add their petitions and thanksgivings, followed by silence
Lord Jesus,
We bow our hearts at your name.

Jesus, we exalt your name in all the world! Bless the dying and the dead. We praise you, that through your death on the cross, you have earned for us everlasting life.
Silence
Lord Jesus,
We bow our hearts at your name.

Christmas 2

The Lord God is both sun and shield; God will give grace and glory. In the house of our God, let us pray, "Lord God of hosts, *hear our prayer.*"

We give thanks for your Church, O God. Bless it with every spiritual blessing in the heavenly places. May we be made happy in the knowledge of the hope to which we are called.
Invite the congregation to add their thanksgivings, followed by silence
Lord God of hosts,
Hear our prayer.

We give thanks for this nation, O God. Give to our leaders a spirit of wisdom. Deliver them from selfish ambition and give all the people a heart for your children, especially those little ones living in poverty or exile.
Silence
Lord God of hosts,
Hear our prayer.

We give thanks for your creation, O God. Where there is desolation, bring forth springs of clean water. Where your creatures are without a place, may they find a place with you.
Silence
Lord God of hosts,
Hear our prayer.

We give thanks for this city, O God. Set us on a straight path where we shall not stumble. Bring new life to languishing areas.
Silence
Lord God of hosts,
Hear our prayer.

We give thanks for all those in our lives, O God. We pray especially for those who know weeping and tears. Turn their mourning into joy, comfort them, and give them gladness for sorrow.
Invite the congregation to add their petitions, followed by silence
Lord God of hosts,
Hear our prayer.

We give thanks for the saints at rest, O God. Gather them into your great heavenly company. May they enjoy forever the riches of your glorious inheritance.
Silence
Lord God of hosts,
Hear our prayer.

Arise, shine; for your light has come, and the glory of the Lord has risen upon you. We pray as pilgrims, "Lead us to your presence; *let us see your glory!*"

Almighty God, grant to your Church wisdom. Work through us that we might lead many to the knowledge and love of you.
Silence
Lead us to your presence;
Let us see your glory!

Defend the needy, Lord Christ. Rescue the poor and thwart all the ways of oppression.
Silence
Lead us to your presence;
Let us see your glory!

The heavens reveal your wonders, O God. Give us eyes to see, hearts to follow, and lives that pay you homage.
Invite the congregation to add their thanksgivings, followed by silence
Lead us to your presence;
Let us see your glory!

Bless all students as they return to school and university. May they find wisdom as well as knowledge; give them a hunger for your truth.
Silence
Lead us to your presence;
Let us see your glory!

Loving God, you are the help of the helpless and the deliverer of those in distress: bless and heal all those in need.
Invite the congregation to add their petitions, followed by silence
Lead us to your presence;
Let us see your glory!

Great redeemer, you have guided us to your presence; you have shown us your glory. Grant us, that we might at last, see you face to face.
Silence
Lead us to your presence;
Let us see your glory!

Epiphany 1A: The Baptism of Our Lord

Ascribe to the Lord the glory due God's name; worship the Lord in the beauty of holiness. Let us pray to the Lord, saying, "In the house of the Lord, all are crying, '*Glory!*"

Lord, give your Church the blessing of peace. Give us the power to testify about your Son, Jesus. Give us your Spirit that we may live fully into your righteous calling.
Silence
In the house of the Lord all are crying,
"*Glory!*"

Lord, give this nation the blessing of peace. Make our hearts understand that you show no partiality, but know that in every nation you accept anyone who does what is right.
Silence
In the house of the Lord all are crying,
"*Glory!*"

Lord, give your creation the blessing of peace. You make yourself known to us in your works. You created the heavens and stretched them out; you spread out the earth and what comes from it. You are upon the mighty waters. Give us the words to witness to your all-encompassing presence.
Silence
In the house of the Lord all are crying,
"*Glory!*"

Lord, give this region the blessing of peace. May we not grow faint until your justice has been established in our hearts and lives.
Silence
In the house of the Lord all are crying,
"*Glory!*"

Lord, give to our friends and family the blessing of peace. Bring your light to those who sit in darkness. In their places of hurt, pain and death, declare new things and spring forth new life.
Invite the congregation to add their petitions and thanksgivings, followed by silence
In the house of the Lord all are crying,
"*Glory!*"

Lord, give to those who have died the blessing of everlasting peace. May those who ate and drank of the body and blood of Christ in this life feast forever in your heavenly kingdom.
Silence
In the house of the Lord all are crying,
"*Glory!*"

Brothers and sisters, grace to you and peace from God our Father and the Lord Jesus Christ. I bid you to come and see the great things God has done. [And God's people say,] *Behold, we come.*

We pray for your Church. Make us a light to the nations. Sanctify us in Christ Jesus, call us to be saints and strengthen us to follow Jesus to the end.
Silence
Come and see the great things God has done.
Behold, we come.

We pray for this nation and the world. May your salvation, O God, reach to the ends of the earth. May all the peoples know of your faithfulness and your deliverance.
Silence
Come and see the great things God has done.
Behold, we come.

We pray for all of creation. Give us a sense of awe as we consider all of the works of your hands.
Invite the congregation to add thanksgivings, followed by silence
Come and see the great things God has done.
Behold, we come.

We pray for our local community. Make our footing sure. Secure for us a future by your love and faithfulness.
Silence
Come and see the great things God has done.
Behold, we come.

We pray for all those in need of your healing and strength. Lift them out of the desolate pit. Put in their mouths a new song of praise. May they know just how great are your wonders and your plans.
Allow the congregation to add their petitions, followed by silence
Come and see the great things God has done.
Behold, we come.

We pray for those who have died. In your great faithfulness, keep them blameless for the day of our Lord Jesus Christ. Honor them in your sight forever.
Silence
Come and see the great things God has done.
Behold, we come.

Epiphany 3A

Friends, in this place, let us behold the fair beauty of our God. With humble hearts let us come before the Lord, saying, "When we call, O Lord, *hearken to our voice.*"

God, help your Church. Heal her divisions. Increase her joy. Unite her members that we might hold as our common purpose to proclaim the gospel.
Silence
When we call, O Lord,
Hearken to our voice.

God, help this nation and the world. Where there are heavy burdens, where oppression reigns, show the strength of your arm and set your people free. We long for the coming of your kingdom.
Silence
When we call, O Lord,
Hearken to our voice.

God, help your creation. You make glorious the way of the sea; you bring us joy at the harvest. Teach us to live in harmony with all you have made.
Invite the congregation to add their thanksgivings, followed by silence
When we call, O Lord,
Hearken to our voice.

God, help our city. May your great light drive away all of the shadows that darken our region. Even now, lift up the heads of the downcast.
Silence
When we call, O Lord,
Hearken to our voice.

God, help the sick and the suffering. Do not forsake them but show yourself to be the strength of their lives and their salvation. By the power of Jesus, heal every disease and sickness among the people.
Invite the congregation to add their petitions, followed by silence
When we call, O Lord,
Hearken to our voice.

God, help the dying and the dead. Hide them in the secrecy of your dwelling. May all those being saved say with boldness, "I belong to Christ forever."
Silence
When we call, O Lord,
Hearken to our voice.

Happy are the ones who put their trust in God! Presenting our prayers and our hearts to God, let us pray, *"Lord God of Hosts, hear our prayer; hearken, O God of Jacob."*

Fill the members of your Church, O God, with a longing and desire for your presence. Fill us with joy as we approach your altar. Sustain us as we go forth in the name of your Christ.
Invite the congregation to add their thanksgivings, followed by silence
Lord God of Hosts, hear our prayer;
Hearken, O God of Jacob.

Bless those, O God, who walk with integrity. Give them the strength to stand for truth in an age of deception and spin.
Silence
Lord God of Hosts, hear our prayer;
Hearken, O God of Jacob.

Almighty God, spring forth new life in desolate places. Restore the beauty and health of your creation.
Silence
Lord God of Hosts, hear our prayer;
Hearken, O God of Jacob.

O Lord, you are both sun and shield. On this city shed your light that we might see our best future. Protect us from the forces of violence and hatred that threaten to undermine the future you want for us.
Silence
Lord God of Hosts, hear our prayer;
Hearken, O God of Jacob.

Merciful and faithful God, we present to you our brothers and sisters who are now in pain and sorrow. We trust them to your mercy, asking that you would heal them.
Invite the congregation to add their petitions, followed by silence
Lord God of Hosts, hear our prayer;
Hearken, O God of Jacob.

Loving God, you sent your Son Jesus to share our human nature, to share our flesh and blood, to share even our suffering and death. We pray for those who suffer and die in the service of others. Grant them your everlasting peace.
Silence
Lord God of Hosts, hear our prayer;
Hearken, O God of Jacob.

God's foolishness is wiser than human wisdom, and God's weakness is stronger than human strength. So let us pray to the Lord, saying, *"For your blessing and guidance, we give you thanks."*

God, bless your Church. May our souls hunger and thirst for righteousness. Give us the grace to do those things you require of us: to do justice, and to love kindness, and to walk humbly with you.
Silence
For your blessing and guidance,
We give you thanks.

God, bless the people of this and every nation. You make foolish the wisdom of the world; we pray that our leaders find their wisdom in you. Teach us to be merciful and open us to receive mercy from others.
Silence
For your blessing and guidance,
We give you thanks.

God, bless your creation. Your mighty, creative voice echoes through the mountains. We offer back to you all the many gifts that spring forth from this earth.
Silence
For your blessing and guidance,
We give you thanks.

God, bless our local community. May we be a people who do no evil to our friends, who heap no contempt upon our neighbors.
Silence
For your blessing and guidance,
We give you thanks.

God, bless the poor in spirit with the inheritance of your kingdom. You choose what is weak in this world to shame the strong. Be the source of life for all those suffering and sick.
Invite the congregation to add their petitions and thanksgivings, followed by silence
For your blessing and guidance,
We give you thanks.

God, bless the dying and the dead. May their reward be great in heaven. Give to those who now mourn the blessing of your comfort.
Silence
For your blessing and guidance,
We give you thanks.

Sisters and brothers, let your light shine before others, so that they may see your good works and give glory to God. Let us pray, "Lord, hear our call, *and answer us.*"

Establish your Church, O God, as a light to the world. Shine your Holy Spirit through us, and all for your glory and the welfare of your people.
Silence
Lord, hear our call,
And answer us.

Righteous God, you delight in justice and mercy: loose the bonds of injustice and let the oppressed go free. Raise up leaders who care for the poor.
Silence
Lord, hear our call,
And answer us.

We thank you, O God, for the gift of light. By it you cause plants to grow; by it you generate warmth; by it you open our eyes to see the beauty of all you have made.
Invite the congregation to add their thanksgivings, followed by silence
Lord, hear our call,
And answer us.

In our own city, Great God, be the restorer of streets. Rebuild our ruined places. May all the people of this community live in security and peace.
Silence
Lord, hear our call,
And answer us.

Be present to all those who cry for help, O Holy One. We pray your healing will spring up quickly for those in need.
Invite the congregation to add their petitions, followed by silence
Lord, hear our call,
And answer us.

The human heart fails to conceive all the good you have prepared for your beloved ones, Heavenly Parent. We trust to you our dying and our dead, believing that you are good and faithful.
Silence
Lord, hear our call,
And answer us.

Happy are they who walk in the law of the Lord! So let us come before the Lord, saying, "Righteous God, *direct our ways.*"

Lord our God, bless your Church. May those who plant and those who water recognize their common purpose. Give abundant growth where your Church labors faithfully.
Silence
Righteous God,
Direct our ways.

Lord our God, bless the people of this and every nation. Draw nations and leaders to choose those ways that promote life and not death.
Silence
Righteous God,
Direct our ways.

Lord our God, bless this planet—your very footstool. Give us the wisdom and will to allow the earth to prosper as you have intended—naturally bringing forth growth and prosperity.
Silence
Righteous God,
Direct our ways.

Lord our God, bless our city. Give us those things we need to live together as neighbors. Remove from our hearts anger, discord, and lust.
Silence
Righteous God,
Direct our ways.

Lord our God, bless the sick and the struggling. May they find life in relationship with you. Make them happy as they seek you with all their hearts.
Invite the congregation to add their petitions and thanksgivings, followed by silence
Righteous God,
Direct our ways.

Lord our God, bless the dying and the dead. May they find peace and comfort at the foot of your heavenly throne.
Silence
Righteous God,
Direct our ways.

Friends, Jesus commends us to, "Be perfect as your heavenly Father is perfect." Therefore, let us come before God, praying, "Incline our hearts, O Lord, to your decrees; *give us life in your ways.*"

Teach your Church, O Lord, to be holy as you are holy. Give us the courage to love our enemies and pray for those who persecute us.
Silence
Incline our hearts, O Lord, to your decrees;
Give us life in your ways.

Teach the people of this and every nation, O Lord, to be about justice and mercy. Help us to treat all people, poor and rich alike, with dignity.
Silence
Incline our hearts, O Lord, to your decrees;
Give us life in your ways.

Teach us, O Lord, to care for your creation. May our fields yield enough to fill the bellies of all who hunger.
Silence
Incline our hearts, O Lord, to your decrees;
Give us life in your ways.

Teach the people of our local community, O Lord, to value each other. May we deal with our neighbors fairly—not holding grudges but loving our neighbors as ourselves.
Silence
Incline our hearts, O Lord, to your decrees;
Give us life in your ways.

Teach the sick and the struggling, O Lord, that you are trustworthy. You have called our bodies holy temples in which your Spirit is pleased to dwell. We pray that where there is sickness, you might bring healing and wholeness.
Invite the congregation to add their petitions and thanksgivings, followed by silence
Incline our hearts, O Lord, to your decrees;
Give us life in your ways.

O Lord, the dying and the dead belong to you. Fulfill your promise to your servants: new and unending life in Christ.
Silence
Incline our hearts, O Lord, to your decrees;
Give us life in your ways.

People of God, wait upon the Lord, from this time forth forevermore. Let us come before our God, praying, "God our provider, *we place our trust in you.*"

Help your Church, O Lord. Keep us and give us as a covenant to the people. May we strive first for your kingdom and your righteousness.
Silence
God our provider,
We place our trust in you.

Help the people of this and every nation, O Lord. Where mountains stand between the people and justice, make of them a road. Quiet tortured souls. We long to see your kingdom come.
Silence
God our provider,
We place our trust in you.

Help us, O Lord, to care for your creation. May the heavens and earth not groan but sing for joy. May we be as mindful of your creatures as you are.
Silence
God our provider,
We place our trust in you.

Help the people of our community, O Lord. May we show our neighbors that you are a generous God who desires to meet all our needs.
Silence
God our provider,
We place our trust in you.

Help the sick and the suffering, O Lord. Comfort those who feel forgotten with the promise spoken through the prophet Isaiah: "I will not forget you. See, I have inscribed you on the palms of my hands."
Invite the congregation to add their petitions and thanksgivings, followed by silence
God our provider,
We place our trust in you.

O Lord, you alone judge the dying and the dead. Have compassion on the dying and give to the dead your commendation. We trust them to you, our Master and Savior.
Silence
God our provider,
We place our trust in you.

When we call upon the Lord, God will answer us. So let us come before the Lord in prayer, saying, "Majestic God, *show us your glory.*"

Lord our God, move your Church by your Holy Spirit. May we proclaim your greatness in the world. Inspire in us a prophetic message and let us not be overcome by fear.
Silence
Majestic God,
Show us your glory.

We pray especially today for our Bishop, [Bishop's name]. May (s)he, like your servant Moses, lead your people into a deeper experience of you.
Silence
Majestic God,
Show us your glory.

O mighty King, lover of justice, may this and every nation strive for justice and peace. We pray that the leaders of the nations trust and care for those in their charge.
Silence
Majestic God,
Show us your glory.

Holy One, you have chosen to wear the clouds and meet our forebears on the mountains. In doing so, you remind us that you created all things good and continue to manifest your glory through those things you have created. Remind us to also honor your creation.
Invite the congregation to add their thanksgivings, followed by silence
Majestic God,
Show us your glory.

O Lord, after they witnessed your majesty, Jesus led his disciples back down the mountain to minister to the people. Lead us to proclaim the Good News of God in Christ to our neighbors—to be your lamps shining in dark places.
Silence
Majestic God,
Show us your glory.

God our Father, touch those who are overcome by fear, sickness or any other adversity. Overshadow them with the healing power of your love.
Invite the congregation to add their petitions, followed by silence
Majestic God,
Show us your glory.

God of Light, we pray for the dying and the dead. May all those who experience death also come to know the new day of resurrection that comes through your Risen Son.
Silence
Majestic God,
Show us your glory.

We do not live by bread alone, but by every word that comes from the mouth of God. Let us pray to the source of our sustenance, saying, "God, our hiding place, *preserve us from trouble.*"

Great God, you have called your people to worship and serve you alone. Instill in us such a singleness of heart that we might perfectly trust you to meet our needs.
Invite the congregation to add their thanksgivings, followed by silence
God, our hiding place,
Preserve us from trouble.

Great God, we live among many temptations. Free the people of this nation, and this world, from all sinful desires that draw us from the love of God.
Silence
God, our hiding place,
Preserve us from trouble.

Great Creator, you have surrounded us with blessings; you provide enough to meet our needs. And yet, we strive and scheme for more, always more. Have mercy on us.
Silence
God, our hiding place,
Preserve us from trouble.

O Lord, we pray for those bound by addiction, those for whom temptation is a constant threat. Set the captives free. Satisfy their cravings with abundant grace.
Silence
God, our hiding place,
Preserve us from trouble.

Be with the sick and suffering, Great Healer. Be for them a hiding place; preserve them from trouble; surround them with shouts of deliverance.
Invite the congregation to add their petitions, followed by silence
God, our hiding place,
Preserve us from trouble.

Through the righteousness of Jesus our Christ, give new and abundant life to all. Justify the dying and the dead. Keep them in your strong hands for ever.
Silence
God, our hiding place,
Preserve us from trouble.

Behold, children of God, it is the Lord who watches over you. As people sent forth into the world let us pray, saying, "Lord, bless us, *so that we may bless others."*

Lord, preserve your Church from all evil. May we, who have been born of water and the Spirit, proclaim the kingdom of God in all the world.
Invite the congregation to add their thanksgiving, followed by silence
Lord, bless us,
So that we may bless others.

O God, may the leaders of the nations ever seek the truth. Open their hearts to true conversion and divine guidance.
Silence
Lord, bless us,
So that we may bless others.

Maker of heaven and earth, you have blessed us with a wondrous and dynamic creation. Protect us from its rage; comfort us by its tranquility. Give us eyes to see your handiwork in the world around us.
Silence
Lord, bless us,
So that we may bless others.

Lord, your eyes never close on your people. We thank you for your mindfulness of us and our community. Be our help and our safety.
Silence
Lord, bless us,
So that we may bless others.

You did not send your Son into the world to condemn the world, but in order that the world may see and experience your salvation. Bring wholeness to those who look to your Son for their help.
Invite the congregation to add their petitions, followed by silence
Lord, bless us,
So that we may bless others.

O God, who gives life to the dead and calls into existence the things that do not exist, keep the dying and the dead from this time forth and for evermore. Give eternal life to all those who trust in you.
Silence
Lord, bless us,
So that we may bless others.

Come, let us bow down, and bend the knee, and kneel before the Lord our Maker. With thankful hearts, let us pray to the Lord saying, "Great God and King, *hear our prayer.*"

Lord, give us eyes to see that the fields are ripe for harvesting. May the Church reap what has been sown by our forebears and sow the seeds that will bring forth the fruit of the future.
Silence
Great God and King,
Hear our prayer.

Lord, reveal the strength of your love to those around the world who are asking, "Is the Lord among us or not?" We pray for comfort and peace for all people.
Silence
Great God and King,
Hear our prayer.

Lord, you hold the caverns of the earth and the heights of the hills; your hands have formed the seas and the dry land. Bless and keep your creation.
Silence
Great God and King,
Hear our prayer.

Lord, where there is suffering in our city, produce endurance; where there is endurance, produce character; where there is character, produce hope. And where we place our hope in you, let us not be disappointed.
Silence
Great God and King,
Hear our prayer.

Lord, we pray for those who are sick or suffering. Give them that living water that comes only through your Son Jesus Christ, that their needs may be met and all their thirsts quenched.
Invite the congregation to add their petitions and thanksgivings, followed by silence
Great God and King,
Hear our prayer.

Lord, we pray for the dying and the dead. We pray in the assurance that all have been reconciled to you through the death of your Son and saved by his new life.
Silence
Great God and King,
Hear our prayer.

Brothers and sisters, live as children of the light—for the fruit of the light is found in all that is good and right and true. Let us pray to the Lord, saying, "Light of the world, *open our eyes.*"

Lord our Shepherd, you have given your Church all that we need. Rain down on us mightily with your Spirit, that we may testify to the astonishing things you have done in our lives.
Invite the congregation to offer their thanksgivings, followed by silence
Light of the world,
Open our eyes.

God, you are present in the valley of the shadow of death. Comfort all those around the world who know danger or violence or war. By your love, cast out all evil and fear.
Silence
Light of the world,
Open our eyes.

Lord, you make us to lie down in green pastures; you lead us by still waters. You have blessed us with a beautiful planet. May we work to preserve the holy gift of nature.
Silence
Light of the world,
Open our eyes.

Lord, spread a table for those who are hungry; where there is scarcity and need in our neighborhoods, fill empty hearts, lives and cups with your abundance. By your light expose all the unfruitful works of darkness.
Silence
Light of the world,
Open our eyes.

God of life, pursue the sick and sorrowful with your goodness and mercy. Reveal your works in those who are suffering. Make yourself known as Healer.
Invite the congregation to add their petitions, followed by silence
Light of the world,
Open our eyes.

Reviver of Souls, give to the dying and the dead your promise of new and unending life. May we one day live with them forever in the light of Christ.
Silence
Light of the world,
Open our eyes.

Brothers and sisters, the Spirit of God dwells in you. Let us appeal to our God, saying, "We call to you, O Lord; *Lord, hear our voice.*"

Breathe new life into your Church, O Lord. Where our bones are dried up, where our hope is lost, cause your life-giving breath to enter. Give us confidence in the truth that the same Spirit that raised Jesus from the dead dwells in us.
Invite the congregation to add their thanksgivings, followed by silence
We call to you, O Lord;
Lord, hear our voice.

Many are they who wait for you, O Lord. Speak into the souls of those suffering throughout the world, a word of hope.
Silence
We call to you, O Lord;
Lord, hear our voice.

Creating God, it is the wind of your Spirit that sweeps across this planet. Renew and refresh your creation; bring forth newness in dead places.
Silence
We call to you, O Lord;
Lord, hear our voice.

With you, O Lord, there is plenteous redemption. Restore the hope of this city. Renew our trust that you have a life-giving future in mind for us.
Silence
We call to you, O Lord;
Lord, hear our voice.

With you, O Lord, there is mercy. Consider well the voice of those who call out from their depths. As they wait for you in their pain and sorrow, give life to their mortal bodies by your healing Spirit.
Invite the congregation to add their petitions, followed by silence
We call to you, O Lord;
Lord, hear our voice.

God, we trust your Son Jesus to be for us resurrection and life. Give to the dead your life. Assure the living with the promise of resurrection.
Silence
We call to you, O Lord;
Lord, hear our voice.

The spirit indeed is willing, but the flesh is weak. So, let us cry out to our Lord, saying, "Crucified King, *have mercy on us.*"

Have mercy on your Church, O Lord, for the times we have denied you. We have not been humble as you are humble. We have been unwilling to share the gospel with our friends and families.
Silence
Crucified King,
Have mercy on us.

Have mercy on those who hold authority in the nations of the world, O Lord—especially those who are threatened by your message of love and justice. Have mercy on us for our silence and complicity.
Silence
Crucified King,
Have mercy on us.

Have mercy on those of us who are called to be stewards of your creation, O Lord. We have exploited and mistreated your masterpiece. Have mercy on us and teach us to love what you have called good.
Silence
Crucified King,
Have mercy on us.

Have mercy on us, O Lord. Teach us to value what you value. Increase in us love for our neighbors.
Silence
Crucified King,
Have mercy on us.

Have mercy on all who are sick and suffering, O Lord. Strengthen those whose strength fails them. Comfort and care for those wasted with grief. Make your face to shine upon your servants.
Invite the congregation to add their petitions and thanksgivings, followed by silence
Crucified King,
Have mercy on us.

Merciful Lord, you know the pain of death—even death on a cross. Have mercy on the dying and the dead. Bring them to the joy of everlasting life in you.
Silence
Crucified King,
Have mercy on us.

Jesus Christ is risen today, our triumphant holy day. Alleluia! So let us pray to our Lord, saying, "Risen Christ, *to you we give undying praise."*

Heavenly King, for us you endured the cross and the grave. When we were yet sinners, you redeemed and saved us. May we sing your eternal praises everywhere we go.
Silence
Risen Christ,
To you we give undying praise.

Incarnate Love, where hearts are wintry, grieving or in pain, call forth new life by your touch. Bring forth life in the barren places of your world.
Silence
Risen Christ,
To you we give undying praise.

Author of Life, you are the ruler of creation. All things created on earth sing to your glory. From the death of the winter, raise the fair beauty of earth.
Silence
Risen Christ,
To you we give undying praise.

Resurrected One, bring our neighbors from sadness into joy. Where they live in darkness, brighten their lives with a day of splendor and give to all that peace that passes human knowing.
Invite the congregation to add their thanksgivings, followed by silence
Risen Christ,
To you we give undying praise.

Triumphant Lord, gladden the faces of all who are sad and fearful-hearted. May they rejoice in your victory over sin and pain—even as they share in your glorious triumph.
Invite the congregation to add their petitions, followed by silence
Risen Christ,
To you we give undying praise.

Risen Christ, you have opened heaven's gate. You have freed us from the power of sin and death. Through your resurrection, you give us the promise of resurrection to a holier state. Bless the dying and the dead.
Silence
Risen Christ,
To you we give undying praise.

Brothers and sisters, peace be with you. Let us pray to our merciful Lord, saying, "Our Lord and our God, *have mercy on us.*"

Lord Jesus Christ, you have given your Church the gift of your Holy Spirit. May that same Spirit comfort and strengthen us as we proclaim your resurrection to the world.
Silence
Our Lord and our God,
Have mercy on us.

God of wisdom, teach and counsel the leaders of the nations. May this world be filled with justice and peace.
Silence
Our Lord and our God,
Have mercy on us.

God our provider, you have given us this pleasant earth as a goodly heritage. May we use its resources wisely and always according to your purpose.
Invite the congregation to add their thanksgivings, followed by silence
Our Lord and our God,
Have mercy on us.

All-knowing God, raise up for this community people who will stand and voice your truth. May we be led by you on good paths of life.
Silence
Our Lord and our God,
Have mercy on us.

Merciful God, you are a strong refuge for those in trouble. Protect all those who suffer various trials. Reveal yourself to those who struggle to believe in you. Make all your people glad by the living hope that is found in you.
Invite the congregation to add their petitions, followed by silence
Our Lord and our God,
Have mercy on us.

God of Life, may the dying and the dead rest in hope. Give us faith that you do not abandon anyone—even to the grave. And preserve us for the great inheritance you give us through the resurrection of your Son from the dead.
Silence
Our Lord and our God,
Have mercy on us.

How shall we repay the Lord for all the good God has done? Let us offers the prayers of our hearts, saying, "Stay with us, Lord Jesus; *and set our hearts on fire.*"

Lord Jesus Christ, you have ransomed us by your own precious blood. Once again, as a holy community, we place our faith and hope in you.
Silence
Stay with us, Lord Jesus;
And set our hearts on fire.

Save us, O Lord, from corruption. Deliver the nations and peoples from greed and hatred. Place in your children hearts of repentance.
Silence
Stay with us, Lord Jesus;
And set our hearts on fire.

O Lord, you are the giver of good things. We thank you for this planet; we thank you for its gifts. We pray a blessing on the seeds that were sown this spring that the harvest might be bountiful.
Invite the congregation to add their thanksgivings, followed by silence
Stay with us, Lord Jesus;
And set our hearts on fire.

O Lord, you are made known in the breaking of bread and so we pray for all those who lack bread. We pray for the hungry. You feed us generously at your table. Help us to generously feed the world.
Silence
Stay with us, Lord Jesus;
And set our hearts on fire.

Whenever we call upon you, gracious Lord, you incline your ear to us. We raise our voices for those for whom we care: those who are ill, those who are struggling, those who are in need of your mercy.
Invite the congregation to add their petitions, followed by silence
Stay with us, Lord Jesus;
And set our hearts on fire.

Precious in your sight, O Lord, is the death of your servants. We trust you with our dead and with our dying. Jesus, be gracious with them, we pray.
Silence
Stay with us, Lord Jesus;
And set our hearts on fire.

Brothers and Sisters, Jesus bore our sins on the cross so that we, free from sins, might live in righteousness. Let us pray to our Lord, saying, "Revive our souls, *and guide us along right pathways.*"

Guardian of our souls, call your Church to greater righteousness. Help us to live by your example and follow in your steps.
Silence
Revive our souls,
And guide us along right pathways.

Guardian of our souls, spread out your table in the presence of those who are troubled. Feed their souls and bodies with your good and generous gifts.
Silence
Revive our souls,
And guide us along right pathways.

Guardian of our souls, you have blessed us with a beautiful planet full of places where we can find rest and peace. May we care for it, as you care deeply for all you have made.
Invite the congregation to add thanksgivings, followed by silence
Revive our souls,
And guide us along right pathways.

Guardian of our souls, you desire the goodwill of all the people. Give us generous hearts and open hands.
Silence
Revive our souls,
And guide us along right pathways.

Guardian of our souls, it is your presence that comforts us. Make your presence known to the sick and the sorrowful, to the fearful and the weak.
Invite the congregation to add their petitions, followed by silence
Revive our souls,
And guide us along right pathways.

Guardian of our souls, you came that we may have life, and have it abundantly. Bring the dying and the dead into your eternal home.
Silence
Revive our souls,
And guide us along right pathways.

Brothers and Sisters, once we were not a people, but now we are God's people. Let us pray to our good God, saying, "Make your face to shine upon us, *and in your loving-kindness save us.*"

In you, O Lord, does your Church take refuge. Strengthen us by your Holy Spirit to do great works in Jesus' name. May your Church glorify you in all our doings.
Silence
Make your face to shine upon us,
And in your loving-kindness save us.

Ancient of Days, rescue the innocent from the hands of those who persecute them. Hold in your strong hands the oppressed and the abused.
Silence
Make your face to shine upon us,
And in your loving-kindness save us.

God, our strong rock, give us eyes to see your hand at work in our world. Lead us and guide us that we may be good stewards of your creation.
Silence
Make your face to shine upon us,
And in your loving-kindness save us.

Tower of Strength, assure those who are unemployed or living in poverty that they are precious in your sight.
Silence
Make your face to shine upon us,
And in your loving-kindness save us.

Merciful God, incline your ear to those in need of deliverance. Calm the troubled hearts of the suffering and the sorrowful, of the sick and the anxiety-plagued.
Invite the congregation to add their petitions and thanksgivings, followed by silence
Make your face to shine upon us,
And in your loving-kindness save us.

God of truth, we commend the dying and the dead into your hands. We rejoice in Jesus' promise that he has prepared for us a place in your eternal home.
Silence
Make your face to shine upon us,
And in your loving-kindness save us.

Bless our God, you peoples; make the voice of God's praise to be heard, saying, "We call out to you with our mouths; *your praise is on our tongues."*

Lord Christ, you have not left us orphaned, but have given your Church an Advocate. May that same Holy Spirit teach us to keep your commandments and comfort us with divine love.
Silence
We call out to you with our mouths;
Your praise is on our tongues.

Loving God, bless the suffering. May those who suffer for doing good find a friend in Christ Jesus. May those who suffer from disasters beyond their control find you attentive to the voice of their prayers.
Silence
We call out to you with our mouths;
Your praise is on our tongues.

Lord of heaven and earth, you made the world and everything in it. You give to all mortals life and breath and all things. May we be faithful stewards of all you have created.
Invite the congregation to add thanksgivings, followed by silence
We call out to you with our mouths;
Your praise is on our tongues.

Merciful Lord, bless the people of this city with a spirit of gentleness and reverence. May we be set free from fear to live, instead, in hope.
Silence
We call out to you with our mouths;
Your praise is on our tongues.

God, you are not far from each one of us. You love us as your children. Reveal your love, especially this day, to the sick and sorrowful.
Invite the congregation to add their petitions, followed by silence
We call out to you with our mouths;
Your praise is on our tongues.

Heavenly Father, you hold our souls in life. You have saved us in baptism. Because your Son Jesus lives so do we rejoice in the hope of unending life in you.
Silence
We call out to you with our mouths;
Your praise is on our tongues.

To our God be the power forever and ever. Amen. Let us appeal to the Lord, saying, "We are yours; *be glorified in us.*"

Holy Father, protect your Church for your name's sake, so that we may be one even as you are one with your Son Jesus and the Holy Spirit. Restore, support, strengthen and establish us and always for your glory.
Silence
We are yours;
Be glorified in us.

Loving God, raise up witnesses to your love in all the world, even to the ends of the earth. Be a parent to orphans, a defender of widows and a provider to the poor.
Silence
We are yours;
Be glorified in us.

Great God of heaven and earth, you graciously send rain to dry places. Give to the people of the earth enough to meet their needs; and yet protect us from dangerous excess. May we acknowledge that all good gifts come from your hand.
Invite the congregation to add thanksgivings, followed by silence
We are yours;
Be glorified in us.

Mighty God, in our own community, exalt the humble in due time. May those who have known suffering and struggle have their dignity renewed. Bless them with gladness. Make their voices heard in shouts of joy. *Silence*
We are yours;
Be glorified in us.

God of all grace, we pray for the lonely and for prisoners, for the sick and the suffering. As they cast their anxieties upon you, may they experience your freedom and care.
Invite the congregation to add their petitions, followed by silence
We are yours;
Be glorified in us.

Heavenly Father, we have been granted eternal life in knowing you through your Son Jesus. Prepare a home for all of the dying and the dead, that they may continue forever in your goodness.
Silence
We are yours;
Be glorified in us.

Peace be with you, brothers and sisters. In wonder and gratitude, let us pray, saying, "You send forth your Spirit: *Come, Holy Spirit.*"

Holy God, by your Spirit you gave birth to your Church: may our many members be the one Body of Christ in this world. Give to each member of your Church the manifestation of the Spirit for the common good.
Silence
You send forth your Spirit:
Come, Holy Spirit.

Holy God, you gave your disciples the ability to speak in the languages of the people: may we also speak about your deeds of power throughout the world, that all may know of your salvation.
Silence
You send forth your Spirit:
Come, Holy Spirit.

Holy God, the earth is full of your creatures: may all who look to you be given food in due season. Open your hand in desolate places and fill the hungry with good things.
Invite the congregation to add thanksgivings, followed by silence
You send forth your Spirit:
Come, Holy Spirit.

Holy God, you poured out your Holy Spirit in your Holy City Jerusalem: pour out your Spirit in our own city. Raise up prophets and dreamers; give us vision.
Silence
You send forth your Spirit:
Come, Holy Spirit.

Holy God, you give the gift of healing by your Spirit: bring healing and wholeness to all those on our hearts and minds this day. You renew the face of the earth; bring renewal to those in need.
Invite the congregation to add their petitions, followed by silence
You send forth your Spirit:
Come, Holy Spirit.

Holy God, we pray for our sisters and brothers who were baptized into the one body, who were made to drink of the one Spirit, and who now have died in Christ. May those who have called upon your name, O Lord, be saved forever.
Silence
You send forth your Spirit:
Come, Holy Spirit.

Trinity Sunday A

Brothers and sisters, live in peace. With gracious hearts appeal to the Lord, saying, "Glory to you, Holy Trinity; *we will praise you and highly exalt you forever.*"

Holy Trinity, you separated the light from the darkness: may your Church ever dwell in your radiance and walk in the light of your love.
Silence
Glory to you, Holy Trinity;
We will praise you and highly exalt you forever.

Holy Trinity, you placed the same sky above all people: may people all over the world live in peace with one another.
Silence
Glory to you, Holy Trinity;
We will praise you and highly exalt you forever.

Holy Trinity, you created all things good: give us the will to respect and preserve your creation, that future generations may experience the goodness of all you have made.
Invite the congregation to add thanksgivings, followed by silence
Glory to you, Holy Trinity;
We will praise you and highly exalt you forever.

Holy Trinity, you created the sun to give us light: shine your light on our city, that the shadow places may be exposed. May your justice and peace reign in our neighborhoods.
Silence
Glory to you, Holy Trinity;
We will praise you and highly exalt you forever.

Holy Trinity, from your hand comes forth creatures great and small: as you care for even the smallest creature, show your loving-kindness to all who call out to you for help. Grace the lives of your children with healing and strength.
Invite the congregation to add their petitions, followed by silence
Glory to you, Holy Trinity;
We will praise you and highly exalt you forever.

Holy Trinity, you created humankind in your image and you promised to be with us always: may those who have died take comfort in your eternal presence.
Silence
Glory to you, Holy Trinity;
We will praise you and highly exalt you forever.

Brothers and sisters, saints of God, Love the Lord! Speak to the Lover of our souls, praying, "Into your hands, O Lord, I commend my spirit; *for you have redeemed me, O Lord, O God of truth."*

God of Truth, put your words in our hearts and souls. May we, without shame, carry your gospel with us where ever we go—and share your love with everyone we meet.
Silence
Into your hands, O Lord, I commend my spirit;
For you have redeemed me, O Lord, O God of truth.

Christ Jesus, by your own righteousness, you are redeeming the world. Rescue our world from sin and destruction. And increase in each of us your love.
Silence
Into your hands, O Lord, I commend my spirit;
For you have redeemed me, O Lord, O God of truth.

O God, you have laid up for us abundant goodness. Your never-ending providence sets in order all things both in heaven and earth. We thank you for your goodness.
Invite the congregation to add thanksgivings, followed by silence
Into your hands, O Lord, I commend my spirit;
For you have redeemed me, O Lord, O God of truth.

We pray for the leaders of our city, O God. Give them wisdom and foresight. May they seek solid foundations rather than the superficial.
Silence
Into your hands, O Lord, I commend my spirit;
For you have redeemed me, O Lord, O God of truth.

Blessed are you, O Lord, you have wondrously shown to us your steadfast love. Preserve your people and hear their cries for help.
Invite the congregation to add their petitions, followed by silence
Into your hands, O Lord, I commend my spirit;
For you have redeemed me, O Lord, O God of truth.

Into you your hands, Gracious Redeemer, do we commit those who have died. Look past their sins and consider your own righteousness. Justify and keep them forever and ever.
Silence
Into your hands, O Lord, I commend my spirit;
For you have redeemed me, O Lord, O God of truth.

Proper 5A

Offer to God a sacrifice of thanksgiving, and pay your vows to the Most High. Call on the Lord, saying, "O God, we long to see your face; *show us your favor.*"

Forgive us, O God. You desire steadfast love and yet too often our hearts are fickle. You long for us to be people of mercy and yet it is much easier to simply go through the motions. Help your Church, O God.
Silence
O God, we long to see your face;
Show us your favor.

God of Abraham, you have made of one blood all the peoples of the earth. Restore us to unity. Help your people, O God.
Silence
O God, we long to see your face;
Show us your favor.

Most High, every wild animal of the forest is yours; all that moves in the field is yours. The world and all that is in it is yours. Make us good stewards of your creation. Help us, O God.
Silence
O God, we long to see your face;
Show us your favor.

Mighty God, come to us like the spring rains that water the earth. Restore this community; refresh its people. Help our city, O God.
Silence
O God, we long to see your face;
Show us your favor.

Holy Jesus, you have come to heal the sick. Heal us. Bind us up. Help those who are suffering, O God.
Invite the congregation to add their petitions and thanksgivings, followed by silence
O God, we long to see your face;
Show us your favor.

Living God, your Holy Child was raised for our justification. We pray for the dead. Raise them up on the last day, that they may live before you in eternity. Help the dying and the dead, O God.
Silence
O God, we long to see your face;
Show us your favor.

My sisters and brothers, worship the Lord with gladness. Let us pray, with joyful hearts, "We give you thanks! *We bless your name!*"

O Lord, you are good; while we were yet sinners Christ died for us. Send us out to share your love. Send your Church out to gather in a plentiful harvest.
Silence
We give you thanks!
We bless your name!

O Lord, you are good; your faithfulness endures to all generations. To those who suffer, give hope. And visit the lonely with your peace.
Silence
We give you thanks!
We bless your name!

O Lord, you are good; all the earth praises you with joyful noise. And we join the song of creation: you are worthy to be praised!
Invite the congregation to add their thanksgivings, followed by silence
We give you thanks!
We bless your name!

O Lord, you are good; you offer us your peace. We pray, Jesus, that you would go about our city—speak a word of good news and healing.
Silence
We give you thanks!
We bless your name!

O Lord, you are good; while we were still weak, Christ died for us. Touch us in our weakness even now. And heal those afflicted with disease or sickness.
Invite the congregation to add their petitions, followed by silence
We give you thanks!
We bless your name!

O Lord, you are good; hope placed in you does not disappoint. We hope for the resurrection of the body and the life everlasting.
Silence
We give you thanks!
We bless your name!

Children of God, praise the Lord! Our God is faithful and hears our prayers, so let us pray, "In your great mercy, O God, *answer us with your unfailing help.*"

To the baptized, O God, grant newness of life. Strengthen us to follow in the footsteps of your Son.
Silence
In your great mercy, O God,
Answer us with your unfailing help.

To the nations of earth, O God of hosts, grant freedom and peace. Deliver the lives of the needy from the hands of evildoers.
Silence
In your great mercy, O God,
Answer us with your unfailing help.

To your created order, O God, grant your help. May the waters, soil, and air be made clean and healthy again.
Invite the congregation to add their thanksgivings, followed by silence
In your great mercy, O God,
Answer us with your unfailing help.

To this city, O God, grant your deliverance. Set us free from violence and destruction. Make safe our streets.
Silence
In your great mercy, O God,
Answer us with your unfailing help.

To those who feel the deep about to swallow them, O God, grant your salvation. In your great compassion, turn to all those in need.
Invite the congregation to add their petitions and thanksgivings, followed by silence
In your great mercy, O God,
Answer us with your unfailing help.

To the dead, O God, grant life eternal with Christ. May all those who have been baptized into the death of Christ be united with him in his resurrection.
Silence
In your great mercy, O God,
Answer us with your unfailing help.

Brothers and sisters, present yourselves to God as those who have been brought from death to life. And with humble hearts, pray to the Lord, saying, "Look upon us; *answer us, O Lord our God.*"

Lord God, you have freed your Church from sin: sanctify us that we may be wholly dedicated to you and your purposes.
Silence
Look upon us;
Answer us, O Lord our God.

Incarnate God, help us to welcome Christ by welcoming the other. Give us eyes to seek and serve Christ in all persons, loving our neighbors as ourselves.
Silence
Look upon us;
Answer us, O Lord our God.

Righteous God, just as you provided a ram for Abraham, you have given us all we need. Encourage us to share what we have so that all may have their needs met.
Invite the congregation to add thanksgivings, followed by silence
Look upon us;
Answer us, O Lord our God.

O Lord, we put our trust in your mercy. We pray you make joyful the hearts of our neighbors—especially the displaced and sorrowful.
Silence
Look upon us;
Answer us, O Lord our God.

O Lord, answer those who cry out in their pain. Comfort those who feel forgotten. Give peace to those who are perplexed and grieving.
Invite the congregation to add their petitions, followed by silence
Look upon us;
Answer us, O Lord our God.

Gracious God, your free gift is eternal life in Christ Jesus our Lord: Bless and keep the dying and the dead.
Silence
Look upon us;
Answer us, O Lord our God.

Thanks be to God through Jesus Christ our Lord! With grateful hearts we pray to our Loving God, saying, "We thank you, Father; *you hear the voice of your beloved.*"

Loving God, you call your Church "my love" and "my beauty." Look upon your Church with eyes of great compassion and love. May we generously share the love with which we have been so greatly blessed.
Invite the congregation to add thanksgivings, followed by silence
We thank you, Father;
You hear the voice of your beloved.

Loving God, you have blessed our nation with great freedoms. Grant us, and all the people of this land, the grace to maintain our liberties in righteousness and peace.
Silence
We thank you, Father;
You hear the voice of your beloved.

Loving God, all that you have created tells of your love for us. May flowers and birds, but even more so our human relationships, remind us of your great care and presence.
Silence
We thank you, Father;
You hear the voice of your beloved.

Loving God, you promise to give rest to all those who carry heavy burdens. Lift up those who are weighed down by the burdens of violence, depression, and despair.
Silence
We thank you, Father;
You hear the voice of your beloved.

Loving God, your Son Jesus revealed your heart to be gentle and humble. We pray for those who have restless souls. We pray that all the sorrowful and the suffering may find their rest in you.
Invite the congregation to add their petitions, followed by silence
We thank you, Father;
You hear the voice of your beloved.

Loving God, you rescue us from death. We pray that all who have died, especially those who strived for freedom and peace, may come to know that heavenly comfort you have prepared for us.
Silence
We thank you, Father;
You hear the voice of your beloved.

Sisters and brothers, you are in the Spirit, since the Spirit of God dwells in you. By that same Spirit let us pray, saying, "Accept, O Lord, the willing tribute of our lips, *and teach us your judgments.*"

Great God, may the word of your kingdom find good soil in your Church. Cause your word to grow in our hearts and bear an abundance of fruit.
Silence
Accept, O Lord, the willing tribute of our lips,
And teach us your judgments.

God of our ancestors, we pray that divided nations be united and warring nations find peace. May we recognize that we are created by your will and are all members of one human family.
Silence
Accept, O Lord, the willing tribute of our lips,
And teach us your judgments.

God of the harvest, bless the seeds and the soil of the world. Give us the wisdom to bring forth its yield wisely and according to your will, that all people may have enough to eat.
Invite the congregation to add their thanksgivings, followed by silence
Accept, O Lord, the willing tribute of our lips,
And teach us your judgments.

Caring God, we are deeply troubled by the gun violence in our city. May all who set their minds on death, even now, be converted to the Spirit of life and peace.
Silence
Accept, O Lord, the willing tribute of our lips,
And teach us your judgments.

Healing God, preserve the lives of the suffering and sick, according to your word. Speak joy into the hearts of the sorrowful.
Invite the congregation to add their petitions, followed by silence
Accept, O Lord, the willing tribute of our lips,
And teach us your judgments.

Eternal God, you preserve all who are in Christ Jesus from condemnation. By the resurrection of your son we trust, that in the fullness of time, you will give life to o mortal bodies through his Spirit that dwells in us.
Silence
Accept, O Lord, the willing tribute of our lips,
And teach us your judgments.

Sisters and brothers, surely the Lord is in this place! So let us cry out to God, saying, "Abba! Father! *Hear our prayer.*"

O Great Parent, you have adopted us as your own children. You have made us joint heirs with Christ. You love us. Lead us by your Spirit and strengthen our hope.
Invite the congregation to add thanksgivings, followed by silence
Abba! Father!
Hear our prayer.

God our King, you have planted us in a complex and often confusing world. Give us patience to live with each other, not judging our neighbors but trusting in your wisdom.
Silence
Abba! Father!
Hear our prayer.

Present God, even creation groans as it waits on you for freedom. Forgive us for the times in which we have subjected it to futility. Give us eyes to see your presence in the heavens, on the earth, and in the seas.
Silence
Abba! Father!
Hear our prayer.

God of Light, darkness is not dark to you. Brighten the places in our city where darkness serves as a cover for crime and violence. Redeem all who are lost.
Silence
Abba! Father!
Hear our prayer.

God of Glory, we wait in hope for the day when we will be set free from the bondage of decay. Even now, free the suffering from pain and the sorrowful from heartache.
vite the congregation to add their petitions, followed by silence
! Father!
r prayer.

may the righteous shine like the sun in your kingdom. We trust that, e, you are with us. In hope, save the dying and the dead.

Sisters and brothers, give thanks to the Lord and call upon God's name! Let us pray to God, saying, "Spirit, help us in our weakness. *Intercede for us.*"

God of the Church, may your people be as persistent as the mustard shrub. May we spread your love and grace to all people and in all places. May we do our kingdom work with the confidence that nothing can separate us from your love.
Silence
Spirit, help us in our weakness.
Intercede for us.

God of the world, make known your deeds among the peoples. Bring peace in places of conflict and violence.
Silence
Spirit, help us in our weakness.
Intercede for us.

God of creation, all of your works are marvelous. Everything in creation with which you have surrounded us speaks to your goodness. Give us eyes to see your fingerprints in our world.
Invite the congregation to add their thanksgivings, followed by silence
Spirit, help us in our weakness.
Intercede for us.

Present God, you did not withhold your own Son, but gave him up for all of us. May we all come to know and experience the depths of your love. By your love, transform hearts and change lives.
Silence
Spirit, help us in our weakness.
Intercede for us.

God of wholeness, neither hardship, nor distress can separate anyone from your love. Assure the suffering and sick, the hurt and sorrowful, that you care for them. May they remember that you are a God who does marvelous things.
Invite the congregation to add their petitions, followed by silence
Spirit, help us in our weakness.
Intercede for us.

God of our ancestors, you have always been mindful of your promises. You promise that not even death can separate us from your love. May all those who have died rest in your eternal love.
Silence
Spirit, help us in our weakness.
Intercede for us.

Friends, God our Savior is our refuge! So let us pray to God, saying, "Incline your ear to us; *hear our words.*"

God our Savior, show us your face. Satisfy your Church in your presence. Reveal to us your ways so that we might walk in the light of your truth.
Silence
Incline your ear to us;
Hear our words.

O God, your eyes are fixed on justice. We pray for all victims of war and violence and famine. Give heed to the cries of those in need throughout the world.
Silence
Incline your ear to us;
Hear our words.

God of abundance, you have blessed the earth with bountiful resources. But we have taken them for granted and mistreated what you made good. Have mercy on us and on our waters. In this time of anxiety, give us eyes to recognize the abundance in our own lives, so that those with little, those who are vulnerable, may also have their fill.
Silence
Incline your ear to us;
Hear our words.

O God, have compassion on the people of our region. Show us your marvelous loving-kindness so that trust in your goodness might replace our fears.
Silence
Incline your ear to us;
Hear our words.

God of blessing, we call upon you, for you answer us in our need. We pray this day for all those desperate for your blessing. Moved by compassion, heal the sick and suffering ones we hold in our hearts this day.
Invite the congregation to add their petitions and thanksgivings, followed by silence
Incline your ear to us;
Hear our words.

God our vindicator, justify the dead through the mercy of your Messiah. We pray that in the fullness of time, they may awake, beholding your likeness.
Silence
Incline your ear to us;
Hear our words.

Sisters and brothers, the word of faith that we proclaim is near you, on your lips and in your heart! So let us pray to God, saying, "Be generous to all who call on you; *Lord, save us."*

Lord God, capture our hearts. May your Holy Spirit prepare a way upon which the beautiful feet of your servants can bring good news to all those who are wearied by too much bad news.
Silence
Be generous to all who call on you.
Lord, save us.

Lord of all, your love makes no distinction between peoples or nations. We pray that wars and violence cease. May your reign of peace and justice come quickly.
Silence
Be generous to all who call on you.
Lord, save us.

Holy God, your Son walked on the water even as your Spirit moved over the face of the waters in creation. May we learn to respect the beauty and mystery, the power and goodness, of all you have made.
Silence
Be generous to all who call on you.
Lord, save us.

Strong God, give us wisdom like your servant Joseph that this congregation may be a symbol of hope and integrity to the leaders of our city.
Silence
Be generous to all who call on you.
Lord, save us.

Lord Christ, you bid your people be not afraid. You have promised that all who call on your name shall be saved. And so make your deeds known among the people—especially those in trouble, sickness and pain.
Invite the congregation to add their petitions and thanksgivings, followed by silence
Be generous to all who call on you.
Lord, save us.

God of our ancestors, by your strength you rescue life even from the depths of the pit. You raised your Son from the grips of death and through him have promised to give new life to all who have died. May the dead rest in peace, even as they await the day of resurrection.
Silence
Be generous to all who call on you.
Lord, save us.

Sisters and brothers, there's a wideness in God's mercy like the wideness of the sea! Therefore let us come before our loving God, saying, "Hear us, we humbly pray; *Lord, help us."*

Loving God, you have shown your Church such great mercy. Through the witness of your Church, may those beyond our walls also experience the goodness of your mercy.
Silence
Hear us, we humbly pray;
Lord, help us.

Lord of all peoples, you have created us to live together. Help us to see that our common life depends on each other's work and goodwill. Cause wars to cease and generosity to prevail.
Silence
Hear us, we humbly pray;
Lord, help us.

Abundant God, you make the earth bring forth good food. As you provided for the children of Israel, we pray you will also provide for all those suffering from famine or need.
Silence
Hear us, we humbly pray;
Lord, help us.

Caring God, how good and pleasant it is when your children live together in unity. Pour out a spirit of reconciliation in our community.
Invite the congregation to add thanksgivings, followed by silence
Hear us, we humbly pray;
Lord, help us.

Lord Christ, may those who call out to you in great faith find your heart open to their cries. We ask for healing for the sick and suffering, the desperate, and disturbed.
Invite the congregation to add their petitions, followed by silence
Hear us, we humbly pray;
Lord, help us.

God of blessing, bless your people with life forevermore. May the dying find comfort; may the dead rest in your peace.
Silence
Hear us, we humbly pray;
Lord, help us.

I appeal to you, brothers and sisters, by the mercies of God, to present your bodies as a living sacrifice, holy, and acceptable to God, which is your spiritual worship. Therefore let us come humbly before God, saying, "Our help is in your name, O Lord; *deal well with us."*

Generous God, you have graciously given the members of your Church diverse gifts: may we, who are many, function in this world as the one body of your Son Jesus Christ.
Silence
Our help is in your name, O Lord;
Deal well with us.

God of the nations, mysterious and unexpected are the instruments of your salvation. Give us eyes to see your work in the lives of the most humble servants and the grandest royalty. Bless all those who put their trust in you.
Silence
Our help is in your name, O Lord;
Deal well with us.

Great God, the maker of heaven and earth, bring forth fruits in due season. May all the people of the world experience the blessing of sun and rain and harvest.
Silence
Our help is in your name, O Lord;
Deal well with us.

Caring God, give to the people of our region sober judgment. May each member of our community live in light of the great mercy you have shown us.
Invite the congregation to add thanksgivings, followed by silence
Our help is in your name, O Lord;
Deal well with us.

Lord God, be on the side of those in need of our prayers. May the sick and sorrowful not be overwhelmed but, instead, find freedom in you.
Allow the congregation to add their petitions and thanksgivings, followed by silence
Our help is in your name, O Lord;
Deal well with us.

Almighty God, you have promised through your beloved Son that not even the gates of Hades will prevail against the people of your redeeming. May all of the dead find comfort in your heavenly kingdom.
Silence
Our help is in your name, O Lord;
Deal well with us.

My sisters and brothers, be kindly affectioned one to another with love. And let us come before God, saying, "We glory in your holy name, *and offer to you our prayer, O Lord."*

Lord Jesus, you bid your disciples take up their cross and follow you: may your holy Church desire, above all, the things of God that we might overcome evil with good.
Silence
We glory in your holy name,
And offer to you our prayer, O Lord.

Lord God of our forebears, you know the sorrows of the afflicted: Deliver those who are being oppressed. And grant your peace to all the world.
Silence
We glory in your holy name,
And offer to you our prayer, O Lord.

Good Lord, you make known your wondrous works: reveal yourself in the works of your hands as even you did to Moses our forebear on the holy mountain.
Invite the congregation to add their thanksgivings, followed by silence
We glory in your holy name,
And offer to you our prayer, O Lord.

O Lord, grant that the people of our land be given to hospitality. May we abhor that which is evil and cleave to that which is good and, in so doing, may we live peaceably one with another.
Silence
We glory in your holy name,
And offer to you our prayer, O Lord.

Strong Lord, make us weep with those who weep. Reveal your strength to the weak and lowly that they may rejoice in all your marvelous works.
Invite the congregation to add their petitions, followed by silence
We glory in your holy name,
And offer to you our prayer, O Lord.

Almighty God, you reward each one according to their works: Give to the dead rest from their labors and life everlasting.
Silence
We glory in your holy name,
And offer to you our prayer, O Lord.

Our Lord Jesus has promised that, when we gather in his name, he is here among us. Let us pray saying, "We are gathered in your name; *accept our prayers.*"

O Lord, you take pleasure in your people: May your Church be a community of honesty and humility. Help us to love each other—especially when love is a challenge.
Silence
We are gathered in your name;
Accept our prayers.

O Lord, you adorn the poor with victory: be with the hungry and the oppressed. Comfort the grieving. Give peace to all whose lives have been upset by natural disaster and war.
Silence
We are gathered in your name;
Accept our prayers.

O Lord, you have caused grapes to grow on the vine and wheat to grow in the fields so that we might celebrate this festive day. Bless the land to grow enough that all people may celebrate its bounty.
Invite the congregation to add their thanksgivings, followed by silence
We are gathered in your name;
Accept our prayers.

O Lord, your Law is summarized, "Love your neighbor as yourself." Help us to love our neighbors so that we might do no wrong by anyone.
Silence
We are gathered in your name;
Accept our prayers.

O Lord, may all those who now lament see the day when they shall sing to you a new song—a song of joy and praise. May those who weep, dance for joy. May the anxious rest on their beds in peace. And may all know that it was you, the Lord, who did this.
Invite the congregation to add their petitions, followed by silence
We are gathered in your name;
Accept our prayers.

O Lord, care for the dead as they await the great day of resurrection. May all who have died rest in your peace.
Silence
We are gathered in your name;
Accept our prayers.

Each of us is finally accountable to God. So let us pray, saying, "Lord, we are in need of your mercy; *have patience with us.*"

Lord, we acknowledge that we all sin against our brothers and sisters in Christ. Forgive us even as we forgive each other. Help us to be merciful to each other in the Church.
Silence
Lord, we are in need of your mercy;
Have patience with us.

Lord, we acknowledge that we desire to repay violence with violence. Open our hearts to forgive even those who commit evil acts towards us and those we love. Help us to live mercifully in our world.
Silence
Lord, we are in need of your mercy;
Have patience with us.

Lord, we acknowledge we do not always appreciate the diversity of your creation. Teach us to live in peace with each other and with your creation. Help us to live mercifully with our world.
Silence
Lord, we are in need of your mercy;
Have patience with us.

Lord, we acknowledge that we do not love our neighbors as you love us. Forgive us for placing ourselves as judge over others when judgment belongs to you alone. Help us to accept the great mercy you choose to show others.
Silence
Lord, we are in need of your mercy;
Have patience with us.

Lord, we pray for those whose lives are broken by evil. Because of your mercy we believe that whatever befalls them, they belong to you; you care for the brokenhearted. Help us to share your love with all those who are hurting.
Invite the congregation to add their petitions and thanksgivings, followed by silence
Lord, we are in need of your mercy;
Have patience with us.

Lord, we remember those who died in violence. We remember those men and women of the armed services, innocent bystanders, first responders, and even those we have called enemies. The dead belong to you, O Lord. Even as we seek your mercy for ourselves, judge all those who have died with mercy.
Silence
Lord, we are in need of your mercy;
Have patience with us.

Sisters and brothers, turn for help to the Lord your strength and constantly seek God's presence. Let us pray to our generous God, saying, "Lead us with gladness, O God; *cover us with shouts of joy!*"

Generous God, you have chosen us to do the work of your kingdom; you have called us to labor in your vineyard. With grateful hearts, we offer to you the best of what we have.
Invite the congregation to add their thanksgivings, followed by silence
Lead us with gladness, O God;
Cover us with shouts of joy!

Generous God, you hear the cry of the hungry. Give bread to all those who face starvation. Use us, as you will, to relieve suffering in our world.
Silence
Lead us with gladness, O God;
Cover us with shouts of joy!

Generous God, you make rivers run in dry places. You have blessed this earth with bountiful resources. Open our eyes to see your hand at work in the world about us.
Silence
Lead us with gladness, O God;
Cover us with shouts of joy!

Generous God, there is enough kingdom work for everyone. Give us eyes to see the opportunities in our own neighborhood. Guide us that we may live in a manner worthy of the gospel of Christ.
Silence
Lead us with gladness, O God;
Cover us with shouts of joy!

Generous God, you hear the cries of the desperate. Marvelous are your works, O God. May the sick and suffering rejoice in you. May the sorrowful call upon your name.
Invite the congregation to add their petitions, followed by silence
Lead us with gladness, O God;
Cover us with shouts of joy!

Generous God, living is Christ and dying is gain. May those who now rest from their labors find their comfort in you. Let light perpetual shine upon them.
Silence
Lead us with gladness, O God;
Cover us with shouts of joy!

Brothers and sisters, in humility regard others as better than yourselves. Humbly then, let us approach our God, saying, "To will and work for your good pleasure, *O Lord, enable us.*"

Christ Jesus, strengthen our tongues to declare you as Lord of our lives. May we, your Church, glorify your Heavenly Parent in word and deed.
Silence
To will and work for your good pleasure,
O Lord, enable us.

Christ Jesus, you chose not to exploit your equality with God, but humbled yourself to be with us. Give us your heart for the marginalized and poor. And may all people, especially those in power, follow your example of humility.
Silence
To will and work for your good pleasure,
O Lord, enable us.

Christ Jesus, by your birth in human likeness you blessed all of creation. Remind us that your feet have trod our soil and tasted our waters. Give us the will to care for this precious planet.
Silence
To will and work for your good pleasure,
O Lord, enable us.

Christ Jesus, you rule the world with love and compassion. Give to our local leaders compassion and vision that the people of our region might live as neighbors, looking out for each other's interests.
Silence
To will and work for your good pleasure,
O Lord, enable us.

Christ Jesus, you became obedient to the point of death that we might have abundant life. Work marvels in the lives of the sick and sorrowful. May they recount to generations the wonderful deeds you have done in their lives.
Invite the congregation to add their petitions and thanksgivings, followed by silence
To will and work for your good pleasure,
O Lord, enable us.

Christ Jesus, through death and resurrection you were highly exalted by God. Continue your good work in those who now rest from their labors. May all the dead find new and lasting life in you.
Silence
To will and work for your good pleasure,
O Lord, enable us.

Sisters and brothers, the law of the Lord is perfect and revives the soul! So let us appeal to our Lord God, saying, "Let the words of our mouths and meditations of our hearts be acceptable in your sight, *O Lord, our strength and our redeemer.*"

Lord our God, you command us to have no other gods before you: give your Church such singleness of mind that we might not be distracted by the rubbish of our lives, but may strive to know Christ and the power of his resurrection.
Silence
Let the words of our mouths and meditations of our hearts be acceptable in your sight,
O Lord, our strength and our redeemer.

Lord our God, you command us to bear not false witness against others: Help us to live in peace with one another. In a world of harmful rhetoric, may we use our words to encourage and love—especially those whom we consider different.
Silence
Let the words of our mouths and meditations of our hearts be acceptable in your sight,
O Lord, our strength and our redeemer.

Lord our God, you command us to keep a holy Sabbath: make us generous stewards of this planet that it may be renewed and refreshed.
Silence
Let the words of our mouths and meditations of our hearts be acceptable in your sight,
O Lord, our strength and our redeemer.

Lord our God, you command us to covet nothing that belongs to our neighbor: give us kind and generous hearts for those with whom we share our neighborhoods. May a loving spirit rule this region.
Silence
Let the words of our mouths and meditations of our hearts be acceptable in your sight,
O Lord, our strength and our redeemer.

Lord our God, you desire that your people be not afraid: Pour on the sick, suffering, and struggling the abundance of your mercy. Bless them with goodness and healing through Jesus the Christ.
Invite the congregation to add their petitions and thanksgivings, followed by silence
Let the words of our mouths and meditations of our hearts be acceptable in your sight,
O Lord, our strength and our redeemer.

Lord our God, you have made us your own: may we, and those who have run the race of faith before us, attain the resurrection from the dead through the abundant mercy of your Son.
Silence
Let the words of our mouths and meditations of our hearts be acceptable in your sight,
O Lord, our strength and our redeemer.

Rejoice in the Lord always; again I will say, Rejoice. Let us humbly approach our God, saying, "Remember us with favor, O Lord; *visit us with your saving help.*"

God our Savior, strengthen your Church to stand firm in your love. May we struggle not *with* one another, but instead struggle *beside* one another in the work of the gospel.
Silence
Remember us with favor, O Lord;
Visit us with your saving help.

God our Savior, you make happy those who act with justice. May the leaders and people of the nations dedicate themselves to pure and honorable dealings. Let your justice reign on this earth.
Silence
Remember us with favor, O Lord;
Visit us with your saving help.

God our Savior, you are good to us. You have blessed us with a rich creation and a beautiful planet for our home. May we cherish the gifts you have given us.
Invite the congregation to add their thanksgivings, followed by silence
Remember us with favor, O Lord;
Visit us with your saving help.

God our Savior, deliver our community from worry. Make us a people of prayer, a congregation who intercedes for our neighbors.
Silence
Remember us with favor, O Lord;
Visit us with your saving help.

God our Savior, you are always near. Assure the lonely; heal the sick; do mighty acts in the lives of the downcast. With thankful hearts, trusting in your mercy, we make our requests known to you.
Invite the congregation to add their petitions, followed by silence
Remember us with favor, O Lord;
Visit us with your saving help.

God our Savior, your mercy endures forever. May those who have died glory in your inheritance and feast at your heavenly banquet for all eternity.
Silence
Remember us with favor, O Lord;
Visit us with your saving help.

Brothers and sisters, beloved by God: Grace to you and peace. Let us pray to the Holy One, saying, "Be gracious to us, O God; *show us your mercy."*

We always give thanks to you, O God, for the Church, constantly remembering before you its work of faith, labor of love, and steadfastness of hope in our Lord Jesus Christ. Inspire us by the Holy Spirit.
Invite the congregation to add their thanksgivings, followed by silence
Be gracious to us, O God;
Show us your mercy.

Almighty God, make us more like your Son, Jesus, who did not regard people with partiality. May we love justice. May we be gracious with all people.
Silence
Be gracious to us, O God;
Show us your mercy.

God our King, the earth shakes in your presence. All that is belongs not to us, but to you. May we be good stewards of all you have created.
Silence
Be gracious to us, O God;
Show us your mercy.

Holy One, you answer those who call upon you. Hear the voices of the weak and wronged. May this city know and experience your presence.
Silence
Be gracious to us, O God;
Show us your mercy.

Great Lord, give your people rest. Cover the sick and sorrowful with your healing hand. May the lonely and forgotten find favor in your sight.
Invite the congregation to add their petitions, followed by silence
Be gracious to us, O God;
Show us your mercy.

Living God, you have rescued the dying and dead from the coming wrath through the death and resurrection of your Christ. May our voices blend with theirs as they proclaim your greatness and worship around your throne forever.
Silence
Be gracious to us, O God;
Show us your mercy.

Proper 25A

Friends, the Lord has been our refuge from one generation to another. Let us pray to our God, saying, "Show your servants your works, O Lord, *and be gracious to us.*"

We pray for the leaders of the Church. Give bishops, priests, deacons, and lay leaders gentle and loving hearts. Empower us to share the gospel and ourselves with those in need.
Silence
Show your servants your works, O Lord,
And be gracious to us.

We pray for all humankind. Prosper the work of our hands. May all those who work earn a fair wage. May those without work find strength and encouragement in your love. Give us hearts to respect the dignity of every human being.
Silence
Show your servants your works, O Lord,
And be gracious to us.

We pray for all creation. You brought forth the mountains. You gave birth to the land and the earth. Give us the desire and will to care for all you have made.
Silence
Show your servants your works, O Lord,
And be gracious to us.

We pray for the areas in which we live. O God, we want to obey what you command. Help us to love our neighbors as ourselves.
Silence
Show your servants your works, O Lord,
And be gracious to us.

We pray for the afflicted and the suffering. And we pray for those who weep and mourn. Nurse them back to health as a mother tenderly nurses her children.
Invite the congregation to add their petitions and thanksgivings, followed by silence
Show your servants your works, O Lord,
And be gracious to us.

We pray for those who have died. Though we are swept away like a dream in this mortal life, you promise to raise us to life immortal through your Son. May your graciousness, O Lord, be upon us.
Silence
Show your servants your works, O Lord,
And be gracious to us.

My brothers and sisters, all who humble themselves will be exalted. So let us appeal to God, praying, "We cry to you, O Lord; *good Lord, deliver us.*"

Humbly we adore you, good Lord. Give to your Church humility. May our lives be pure, upright and blameless; may we, in word and deed, proclaim your gospel.
Silence
We cry to you, O Lord;
Good Lord, deliver us.

Humbly we adore you, good Lord. Give to this nation humility. May we find our greatness not in status or self-exaltation, but in service to others.
Silence
We cry to you, O Lord;
Good Lord, deliver us.

Humbly we adore you, good Lord. Teach us to handle your creation with humility. Bless the soil to bring forth a fruitful harvest for the hungry. Bless the springs to give drink for the thirsty.
Silence
We cry to you, O Lord;
Good Lord, deliver us.

Humbly we adore you, good Lord. Give to our city humility. You have blessed us with a good place in which to dwell. Renew the spirits of our languishing. Put songs of thanksgiving in our mouths.
Invite the congregation to add their thanksgivings, followed by silence
We cry to you, O Lord;
Good Lord, deliver us.

Humbly we adore you, good Lord. Give healing and strength to those who call to you from humble hearts. Lift the burdens of those who are heavy laden. Encourage the sick and sorrowful with your love.
Invite the congregation to add their petitions, followed by silence
We cry to you, O Lord;
Good Lord, deliver us.

Humbly we adore you, good Lord. Your mercy endures forever. Bring those who have walked through the waters of baptism into that place of eternal life and promise.
Silence
We cry to you, O Lord;
Good Lord, deliver us.

All Saints' Day A (or the Sunday closest)

Alleluia! Let us join the countless throngs who sing God's praises, praying, "We bless, O Lord; *your praise is ever in our mouths.*"

God of the pilgrim Church, you love us and call us your children: give your Church a hunger and a thirst for righteousness. Continue to nurture us by the example and fellowship of those saints who have journeyed before us.
Silence
We bless, O Lord;
Your praise is ever in our mouths.

God of all people, you love us and call us your children: In a world of violence and war, you bless the peacemakers. Make us instruments of healing and peace.
Silence
We bless, O Lord;
Your praise is ever in our mouths.

God of creation, you love us and call us your children: you have given this earth to the meek. May our steps be gentle and leave a small footprint on our earth. As it has been handed on to us, may we carefully preserve this creation for future generations.
Silence
We bless, O Lord;
Your praise is ever in our mouths.

God of the city, you love us and call us your children: bless the poor with good things. Visit our impoverished neighborhoods with hope, mercy, and relief. Give us hearts for the poor in our region.
Silence
We bless, O Lord;
Your praise is ever in our mouths.

God of the mournful and suffering, you love us and call us your children: comfort and heal those in need. Hear them in their affliction and save them from their troubles.
Invite the congregation to add their petitions, followed by silence
We bless, O Lord;
Your praise is ever in our mouths.

God of the Church at rest, you love us and call us your children: we praise you for the faith and witness of all the saints. May their prayers and presence continue to strengthen us. It is with their triumphant voices that we join our own prayers and praises. Alleluia!
Invite the congregation to add their thanksgivings, followed by silence
We bless, O Lord;
Your praise is ever in our mouths.

Brothers and sisters, Christ will come again! In hope let us make our prayer, "You are our help and our deliverance; *Come quickly, Lord.*"

Open wide your doors to us, O Lord. Accept us into your Kingdom. Give your Church endurance that we might keep our eyes open and fixed on you.
Silence
You are our help and our deliverance;
Come quickly, Lord.

Let justice roll down like waters and righteousness like an everflowing stream. Drown the evil of our times in a flood of mercy. Refresh the needy with the abundance of your love.
Silence
You are our help and our deliverance;
Come quickly, Lord.

God of the harvest, inspire our hearts to care deeply for your creation. Help us to live and work in harmony with all you have made.
Silence
You are our help and our deliverance;
Come quickly, Lord.

God, raise up leaders in our community. Bless them with wisdom. Give us hope and a future.
Invite the congregation to add their thanksgivings, followed by silence
You are our help and our deliverance;
Come quickly, Lord.

Be pleased, O God, to deliver those in need. Make haste to help the troubled. You are a great God and with you is health and salvation. We trust our loved ones to you.
Invite the congregation to add their petitions, followed by silence
You are our help and our deliverance;
Come quickly, Lord.

Through the death and resurrection of your Son, you give us new and unending life. We trust our dead to you, Merciful God.
Silence
You are our help and our deliverance;
Come quickly, Lord.

Brothers and sisters, in love let us encourage one another and build each other up. Let us pray saying, "Have mercy upon us, O Lord, *have mercy.*"

Lord God, you have destined us not for wrath but for obtaining salvation through our Lord Jesus Christ: strengthen your Church to confidently share your gospel throughout the world.
Silence
Have mercy upon us, O Lord,
Have mercy.

Lord God, have mercy on all who are shown contempt and scorn: Hear the cries of the needy and lift up the downtrodden and lowly.
Silence
Have mercy upon us, O Lord,
Have mercy.

Lord God, you rule the day and the night: Bless and sustain the works of your hands. Restore your creation.
Silence
Have mercy upon us, O Lord,
Have mercy.

Lord God, you are enthroned in the heavens: may we trust not our own schemes but lift up our eyes to you. Lead and guide our city and its leaders in all justice and truth.
Silence
Have mercy upon us, O Lord,
Have mercy.

Lord God, you are a merciful God: hear the prayers of those who cry out to you for help. Be present with the suffering in their waking and their sleeping.
Invite the congregation to add their petitions and thanksgivings, followed by silence
Have mercy upon us, O Lord,
Have mercy.

Lord God, your Son Jesus died for us that we might dwell in your light forever: give to the dying and the dead the hope of salvation.
Silence
Have mercy upon us, O Lord,
Have mercy.

Serve the Lord with gladness and come before God's presence with a song. Let us pray together, saying, "We give you thanks, O Lord; *and call upon your Name."*

Christ the King, you have been made head over all things for the Church: may we worthily live as your body in our world. Work your great power in and through us.
Silence
We give you thanks, O Lord;
And call upon your Name.

Christ the King, you gather all the nations of the world to yourself: bless the world's suffering with your everlasting mercy. May the oppressed be fed with your justice.
Silence
We give you thanks, O Lord;
And call upon your Name.

Christ the King, it is from your hand that all are fed: inspire righteousness in all people that the hungry may be fed and the thirsty given clean water to drink.
Silence
We give you thanks, O Lord;
And call upon your Name.

Christ the King, you care for those in prison: give us hearts for all those who are incarcerated. Where there is crime and violence in our city, offer your peace.
Silence
We give you thanks, O Lord;
And call upon your Name.

Christ the King, you are good: we pray you seek the lost, bind up the injured, and strengthen the weak.
Invite the congregation to add their petitions and thanksgivings, followed by silence
We give you thanks, O Lord;
And call upon your Name.

Christ the King, your faithfulness endures from age to age: may all your saints, at work and at rest, know the hope to which you have called us and the riches of your glorious inheritance.
Silence
We give you thanks, O Lord;
And call upon your Name.

YEAR B

Brothers and sisters, what I say to you I say to all: keep awake. Let us appeal to God, saying, "Show the light of your countenance, *and we shall be saved.*"

Restore your holy catholic Church, O Lord God of hosts. Give us eyes to see that together we are not lacking any spiritual gift. Strengthen us that we may be blameless on the day of our Lord Jesus Christ.
Silence
Show the light of your countenance,
And we shall be saved.

Restore justice throughout the world, O Lord God of hosts. You work for those who wait for you. Come to the help of the oppressed and the needy.
Silence
Show the light of your countenance,
And we shall be saved.

Restore your creation, O Lord God of hosts. Awesome are your deeds and wonderful are the works of your hands.
Invite the congregation to add their thanksgivings, followed by silence
Show the light of your countenance,
And we shall be saved.

Restore peace in the city, O Lord God of hosts. Make us mindful of our interdependence. Help us to respect the dignity of our neighbors.
Silence
Show the light of your countenance,
And we shall be saved.

Restore the weak to strength, O Lord God of hosts. Come quickly with healing in your wings.
Invite the congregation to add their petitions, followed by silence
Show the light of your countenance,
And we shall be saved.

Restore our hope, O Lord God of hosts. Though we all fade like a leaf, still you are faithful. You have called your people into the fellowship of your Son forever.
Silence
Show the light of your countenance,
And we shall be saved.

Advent 2B

Sisters and brothers in Christ, strive to be found by God at peace, without spot, or blemish. Placing our trust in God, let us pray, "Gather us in your arms; *carry us in your heart.*"

O God, we pray for the Church. May those who have been baptized with water and the Holy Spirit live no longer in their sins but lead lives of holiness and godliness.
Silence
Gather us in your arms;
Carry us in your heart.

O God, we pray for the nations of the world. May your voice be heard in all the earth, your glory revealed in all lands. Rain down righteousness and peace in abundance.
Silence
Gather us in your arms;
Carry us in your heart.

O God, we pray for the creation. Continually renew the heavens and the earth by your mercy.
Silence
Gather us in your arms;
Carry us in your heart.

O God, we pray for our community. We long to see truth spring up through the frozen earth and be found in all our hearts and minds.
Silence
Gather us in your arms;
Carry us in your heart.

O God, we pray for the sick and the sorrowful. Comfort the suffering with your tenderness. Speak peace to your people.
Invite the congregation to add their petitions and thanksgivings, followed by silence
Gather us in your arms;
Carry us in your heart.

O God, we pray for those who have died. Though we mortals fade like the flowers, still you gently lead the dead into your heavenly home to dwell with your saints forever.
Silence
Gather us in your arms;
Carry us in your heart.

Dear friends, hold fast to what is good. And let us praise our God, saying, "We rejoice in you, O Lord; *we exult in you.*"

We rejoice in you, O God: you have clothed your people with the garments of salvation; you have covered us with robes of righteousness. You have done great things for us.
Invite the congregation to add their thanksgivings, followed by silence
We rejoice in you, O Lord;
We exult in you.

We rejoice in you, O God: you are a lover of justice. May your kingdom come and your will be done on earth. Replace your children's tears with laughter.
Silence
We rejoice in you, O Lord;
We exult in you.

We rejoice in you, O God: you cause the seeds to grow and the earth to bring forth its shoots. May the fields and streams, mountains and oceans, glorify you.
Silence
We rejoice in you, O Lord;
We exult in you.

We rejoice in you, O God: you are the repairer of cities. Build up ruined places, raise up whatever is devastated. Heal our city.
Silence
We rejoice in you, O Lord;
We exult in you.

We rejoice in you, O God: you speak good news to the oppressed, the brokenhearted, the captive, and those who mourn. May those who sow with tears, reap with songs of joy.
Invite the congregation to add their petitions, followed by silence
We rejoice in you, O Lord;
We exult in you.

We rejoice in you, O God: through your Son, Jesus the Christ, you have made an everlasting covenant with us. Bless the dying and the dead forever.
Silence
We rejoice in you, O Lord;
We exult in you.

Sisters and brothers, the Lord is with you! Let us pray to the Almighty, saying, "My soul proclaims your greatness, O Lord; *our spirits rejoice in you!*"

God our Savior, give to your Church the humble heart of Mary. In our lives and ministries, let it be with us according to your word.
Silence
My soul proclaims your greatness, O Lord;
Our spirits rejoice in you!

God our Savior, give grace to your bishops, priests, and deacons. Strengthen all your ministers according to the proclamation of Jesus Christ.
Silence
My soul proclaims your greatness, O Lord;
Our spirits rejoice in you!

God our Savior, you cast down the mighty from their thrones and lift up the lowly. May both the mighty and the lowly, and all those in-between, experience the amazing depth of your great mercy.
Silence
My soul proclaims your greatness, O Lord;
Our spirits rejoice in you!

God our Savior, you long for the hungry to be filled with good things. Bless us to work with you to bring forth good food and drink from your precious earth.
Silence
My soul proclaims your greatness, O Lord;
Our spirits rejoice in you!

God our Savior, we ask you to do great things in our city, in our neighborhoods, in our region.
Invite the congregation to add their thanksgivings, followed by silence
My soul proclaims your greatness, O Lord;
Our spirits rejoice in you!

God our Savior, you ever remember your promise of mercy. Be merciful to the lonely, despised, sorrowful, and sick. Speak good news into sad hearts; come to the help of the needy.
Invite the congregation to add their petitions, followed by silence
My soul proclaims your greatness, O Lord;
Our spirits rejoice in you!

God our Savior, nothing is impossible with you. May all those who have died find a place in the eternal kingdom of your Christ.
Silence
My soul proclaims your greatness, O Lord;
Our spirits rejoice in you!

Come let us adore Christ, the Lord. Let us pray: "Glorious Lord, *grant us your peace.*"

Christ the Lord, we humbly adore you: Make joyful our hearts. Strengthen your Church with humility and faith that we might triumph over the power of evil.
Silence
Glorious Lord,
Grant us your peace.

Christ the Lord, we humbly adore you: you abhor neither the simple nor the lowly. Shine your light on all the world that the nations may look upon your truth and find their salvation.
Silence
Glorious Lord,
Grant us your peace.

Christ the Lord, we humbly adore you: may all of creation burst forth in songs of praise. May all the works of your hand glorify you.
Invite the congregation to add their thanksgivings, followed by silence
Glorious Lord,
Grant us your peace.

Christ the Lord, we humbly adore you: summon the people of the city to yourself. May all of the distractions and heartache of our lives fade away in the joy of your presence.
Silence
Glorious Lord,
Grant us your peace.

Christ the Lord, we humbly adore you: you love us so dearly. Grant your healing grace to sinners, to the poor, to those in need of love. Open your arms to the sick and the lonely.
Invite the congregation to add their petitions, followed by silence
Glorious Lord,
Grant us your peace.

Christ the Lord, we humbly adore you: all glory be given to you. You blessed our earthly bodies with your birth; and you promise to raise us to new life by your death and resurrection.
Silence
Glorious Lord,
Grant us your peace.

Christmas 1

The Word became flesh and lived among us, and we have seen his glory, the glory as of a father's only son, full of grace and truth. We are witnesses, praying, "Shine forth in our lives, O Lord. *Hallelujah!*"

Abba, Father, you have received us as your children. Make our hearts shine ever brighter with the pure light of Christ, that all people might witness your all-encompassing love.
Silence
Shine forth in our lives, O Lord.
Hallelujah!

Almighty God, let all the nations witness your glory. Cause righteousness and praise to cover the earth.
Silence
Shine forth in our lives, O Lord.
Hallelujah!

Great Lord, you are mighty in power: you graciously make the earth to burst forth with green plants; you provide food for flocks and herds; you give us the resources to thrive on this planet. May we be thankful in our hearts and generous in our lives.
Invite the congregation to add their thanksgivings, followed by silence
Shine forth in our lives, O Lord.
Hallelujah!

O God, it is you who establishes peace. Comfort your people with safety and security; assure us that it is not by our own strength, but by your goodness, that we can rest in quiet confidence.
Silence
Shine forth in our lives, O Lord.
Hallelujah!

Loving God, you are the healer of the brokenhearted; it is you who binds up their wounds; you lift up the lowly. Clothe your children with the garments of health and salvation.
Invite the congregation to add their petitions, followed by silence
Shine forth in our lives, O Lord.
Hallelujah!

O God, you sent your Son to redeem us from sin and death: draw us closer to your Son Jesus—into your heart, both now and in the life to come.
Silence
Shine forth in our lives, O Lord.
Hallelujah!

Sisters and brothers, let the same mind be in you that was in Christ Jesus. With humble hearts let us say to the Lord, "Lord Jesus, *we bow our hearts at your name.*"

Jesus, we exalt your name in all the world! Bless your Church. Inspire us by the Holy Spirit to confess you as Lord over all we are, all we do and all we hope to do.
Silence
Lord Jesus,
We bow our hearts at your name.

Jesus, we exalt your name in all the world! Bless the people of the world. May the whole world experience your peace.
Silence
Lord Jesus,
We bow our hearts at your name.

Jesus, we exalt your name in all the world! Bless our planet. Make us faithful stewards of all the works of your fingers. Forgive us when we fail to respect your creatures: the beasts of the field, the birds of the air, and the fish of the sea.
Silence
Lord Jesus,
We bow our hearts at your name.

Jesus, we exalt your name in all the world! Bless our city and our region. Give us renewed hope and purpose as we begin this new year.
Silence
Lord Jesus,
We bow our hearts at your name.

Jesus, we exalt your name in all the world! Bless the sick and the lonely and all those in great need. Make your face to shine on them and be gracious to them.
Invite the congregation to add their petitions and thanksgivings, followed by silence
Lord Jesus,
We bow our hearts at your name.

Jesus, we exalt your name in all the world! Bless the dying and the dead. We praise you that through your death on the cross you have earned for us everlasting life.
Silence
Lord Jesus,
We bow our hearts at your name.

The Lord God is both sun and shield; God will give grace and glory. In the house of our God, let us pray, "Lord God of hosts, *hear our prayer.*"

We give thanks for your Church, O God. Bless it with every spiritual blessing in the heavenly places. May we be made happy in the knowledge of the hope to which we are called.
Invite the congregation to add their thanksgivings, followed by silence
Lord God of hosts,
Hear our prayer.

We give thanks for this nation, O God. Give to our leaders a spirit of wisdom. Deliver them from selfish ambition and give all the people a heart for your children, especially those little ones living in poverty or exile.
Silence
Lord God of hosts;
Hear our prayer.

We give thanks for your creation, O God. Where there is desolation, bring forth springs of clean water. Where your creatures are without a place, may they find a place within you.
Silence
Lord God of hosts,
Hear our prayer.

We give thanks for this city, O God. Set us on a straight path where we shall not stumble. Bring new life to languishing areas.
Silence
Lord God of hosts,
Hear our prayer.

We give thanks for all those in our lives, O God. We pray especially for those who know weeping and tears. Turn their mourning into joy, comfort them, and give them gladness for sorrow.
Invite the congregation to add their petitions, followed by silence
Lord God of hosts,
Hear our prayer.

We give thanks for the saints at rest, O God. Gather them into your great heavenly company. May they enjoy forever the riches of your glorious inheritance.
Silence
Lord God of hosts,
Hear our prayer.

Arise, shine; for your light has come, and the glory of the Lord has risen upon you. We pray as pilgrims, "Lead us to your presence; *let us see your glory!"*

Almighty God, grant to your Church wisdom. Work through us that we might lead many to the knowledge and love of you.
Silence
Lead us to your presence;
Let us see your glory.

Defend the needy, Lord Christ. Rescue the poor and thwart all the ways of oppression.
Silence
Lead us to your presence;
Let us see your glory.

The heavens reveal your wonders, O God. Give us eyes to see, hearts to follow, and lives that pay you homage.
Invite the congregation to add their thanksgivings, followed by silence
Lead us to your presence;
Let us see your glory.

Bless all students as they return to school and university. May they find wisdom as well as knowledge; give them a hunger for your truth.
Silence
Lead us to your presence;
Let us see your glory.

Loving God, you are the help of the helpless and the deliverer of those in distress: bless and heal all those in need.
Invite the congregation to add their petitions, followed by silence
Lead us to your presence;
Let us see your glory.

Great redeemer, you have guided us to your presence; you have shown us your glory. Grant us, that we might at last, see you face to face.
Silence
Lead us to your presence;
Let us see your glory.

Epiphany 1B: The Baptism of Our Lord

Sisters and brothers, ascribe to the Lord the glory due God's name. Let us approach our great God with humble hearts saying: "Lord, give strength to your people; *bless us with peace."*

Lover of souls, you seal us by your Holy Spirit in baptism and claim us as your own forever: may our offering of worship be acceptable in your sight.
Silence
Lord, give strength to your people;
Bless us with peace.

Lover of souls, you sit enthroned as king for evermore: may the leaders of the nations do justice and govern with mercy.
Silence
Lord, give strength to your people;
Bless us with peace.

Lover of souls, you created the heavens and the earth: we praise you that you make holy such basic things of earth—water for baptism, grapes and grain to sustain our souls.
Invite the congregation to add their thanksgivings, followed by silence
Lord, give strength to your people;
Bless us with peace.

Lover of souls, you forgive the sins of the penitent and care for the injured: be with all victims of gun violence; heal and convert the hearts of the violent. May our city know peace.
Silence
Lord, give strength to your people;
Bless us with peace.

Lover of souls, your voice is a voice of splendor: speak healing and comfort to all the heartbroken and needy.
Invite the congregation to add their petitions, followed by silence
Lord, give strength to your people;
Bless us with peace.

Lover of souls, you called the light into being: let light perpetual shine on those who have died. May we all rest in the hope of life eternal.
Silence
Lord, give strength to your people;
Bless us with peace.

Sisters and brothers, you were bought with a price. So let us offer ourselves to God, praying: "God, you call us; *give us ears to listen.*"

Holy God, you call your Church to share the good news of your love: we pray especially this day for our parish. We ask that you inspire us to do the work you have called us to do. Create in us generous hearts and willing spirits.
Silence
God, you call us;
Give us ears to listen.

Holy God, you call the nations to yourself: open our eyes to see the goodness, and respect the dignity, of every human being. May we recognize that your goodness has no boundary or limitation.
Silence
God, you call us;
Give us ears to listen.

Holy God, you call us to care for your creation: your works are wonderful. Open our eyes to the beauty of our world so that we might better tend to our planet.
Invite the congregation to add their thanksgivings, followed by silence
God, you call us;
Give us ears to listen.

Holy God, you have made our bodies a temple for your Holy Spirit: we pray for all victims of physical and sexual abuse. Heal and glorify broken bodies that, being made whole by your love, they may glorify you.
Silence
God, you call us;
Give us ears to listen.

Holy God, you search us out and know us: comfort and heal the sick and sorrowful that they may know they are not alone. Keep them ever on your mind and in your thoughts.
Allow the congregation to add their petitions, followed by silence
God, you call us;
Give us ears to listen.

Holy God, if we climb up to heaven, you are there; when we make the grave our bed, you are there also. Hold the dead in your heart forever and comfort the living with hope eternal.
Silence
God, you call us;
Give us ears to listen.

Put your trust in God always, O people. With humble hearts let us pray to God: "Steadfast love is yours, O Lord; *show us mercy.*"

O God, you have called your Church to be merciful. May your Church be known by the love we show and the grace we speak. Our souls in silence wait for you.
Silence
Steadfast love is yours, O Lord;
Show us mercy.

O God, you love those we call enemy. Transform our hearts that we might not wish for the destruction of any but instead hope for the salvation of all people. Our souls in silence wait for you.
Silence
Steadfast love is yours, O Lord;
Show us mercy.

O God, we recognize that we take your creation for granted. Forgive us and teach us to be good stewards. Our souls in silence wait for you.
Silence
Steadfast love is yours, O Lord;
Show us mercy.

O God, we lift to you the hungry and poor of our region. We ask you to be for them a strong rock and refuge. Our souls in silence wait for you.
Silence
Steadfast love is yours, O Lord;
Show us mercy.

O God, in you is our safety and honor. Bless those who are sick and those who are brokenhearted. Give to all the comfort of your peace. Our souls in silence wait for you.
Invite the congregation to add their petitions and thanksgivings, followed by silence
Steadfast love is yours, O Lord;
Show us mercy.

O God, even while this life is passing away, you are faithful. Receive into your heavenly kingdom the dying and the dead. Continue to bless them with your love. Our souls in silence wait for you.
Silence
Steadfast love is yours, O Lord;
Show us mercy.

Happy are the ones who put their trust in God! Presenting our prayers and our hearts to God, let us pray, "Lord God of Hosts, hear our prayer; *hearken, O God of Jacob.*"

Fill the members of your Church, O God, with a longing and desire for your presence. Fill us with joy as we approach your altar. Sustain us as we go forth in the name of your Christ.
Invite the congregation to add their thanksgivings, followed by silence
Lord God of Hosts, hear our prayer;
Hearken, O God of Jacob.

Bless those, O God, who walk with integrity. Give them the strength to stand for truth in an age of deception and spin.
Silence
Lord God of Hosts, hear our prayer;
Hearken, O God of Jacob.

Almighty God, spring forth new life in desolate places. Restore the beauty and health of your creation.
Silence
Lord God of Hosts, hear our prayer;
Hearken, O God of Jacob.

O Lord, you are both sun and shield. On this city shed your light that we might see our best future. Protect us from the forces of violence and hatred that threaten to undermine the future you want for us.
Silence
Lord God of Hosts, hear our prayer;
Hearken, O God of Jacob.

Merciful and faithful God, we present to you our brothers and sisters who are now in pain and sorrow. We trust them to your mercy, asking that you would heal them.
Invite the congregation to add their petitions, followed by silence
Lord God of Hosts, hear our prayer;
Hearken, O God of Jacob.

Loving God, you sent your Son Jesus to share our human nature, to share our flesh and blood, to share even our suffering and death. We pray for those who suffer and die in the service of others. Grant them your everlasting peace.
Silence
Lord God of Hosts, hear our prayer;
Hearken, O God of Jacob.

Epiphany 4B

Brothers and sisters, the fear of the Lord is the beginning of wisdom. Let us appeal to the Lord, saying: "You are gracious and full of compassion, O Lord; *hear our prayer.*"

O Lord, you have made the Church a family through the waters of baptism: let us not sin against each other but instead build each other up in love.
Silence
You are gracious and full of compassion, O Lord;
Hear our prayer.

O Lord, the works of your hands are faithfulness and justice: may the nations of the world be ruled by truth and equity. Give us a vision for peace.
Silence
You are gracious and full of compassion, O Lord;
Hear our prayer.

O Lord, all things are from you and exist for you: give us ears to heed the words spoken on behalf of our planet; and give us the will to be faithful stewards.
Silence
You are gracious and full of compassion, O Lord;
Hear our prayer.

O Lord, you sent your son to set us free from the unclean spirits that harass your people: set us free from the violence in our land, especially gun violence. In your compassion, cast out hatred and anger.
Silence
You are gracious and full of compassion, O Lord;
Hear our prayer.

O Lord, you know those who love you: show all the sick and suffering your marvelous works. Fill their hearts with songs of praise.
Invite the congregation to add their petitions and thanksgivings, followed by silence
You are gracious and full of compassion, O Lord;
Hear our prayer.

O Lord, you have redeemed your people: remember your covenant and care for your children forever, even beyond death and the grave.
Silence
You are gracious and full of compassion, O Lord;
Hear our prayer.

Brothers and sisters, how pleasant it is to honor God with praise! Let us pray to the Lord, saying: "Great are you, O Lord; *Hallelujah!*"

O God, your Son Jesus came into the world to proclaim your message. Give your Church, the body of Christ, that same passion to be all things to all people that we might show forth your salvation.
Silence
Great are you, O Lord;
Hallelujah!

O God, you cast the wicked to the ground and lift up the lowly. Protect and defend those living under oppressive rulers and those living under the oppression of hunger, poverty, and war.
Silence
Great are you, O Lord;
Hallelujah!

O God, you prepare rain for the earth and make grass to grow on the plains and hills. Provide food enough to support all the creatures that inhabit the earth.
Silence
Great are you, O Lord;
Hallelujah!

O God, there is no limit to your wisdom; your understanding is unsearchable. Bless all teachers and students. Sustain our school systems and universities. Bless your people with knowledge.
Invite the congregation to add their thanksgivings, followed by silence
Great are you, O Lord;
Hallelujah!

O God, you give power to the faint and strengthen the powerless. In the name of Jesus, we ask that you heal those with diseases and set free those in bondage. Heal the brokenhearted and care for the wounded.
Invite the congregation to add their petitions, followed by silence
Great are you, O Lord;
Hallelujah!

O God, you are everlasting, the creator of the ends of the earth. We entrust to your tireless care those who have died.
Silence
Great are you, O Lord;
Hallelujah!

Sing to the Lord, you servants of the Lord! With thankful hearts, let us pray: "Hear, O Lord; *have mercy upon us."*

Healing God, give us hearts to love the lonely; give us hands to touch the hurting; give us courage to speak your grace to the suffering. Build your Church into a place of new life.
Silence
Hear, O Lord;
Have mercy upon us.

God of Elisha, raise up prophets to speak healing into the relationships of the nations. May we see an end to war; may the captives be set free.
Silence
Hear, O Lord;
Have mercy upon us.

God of creation, you give us water to make us clean, to refresh our bodies. We pray that you refresh the waters, forgiving us for our neglect and misuse of your precious gift.
Silence
Hear, O Lord;
Have mercy upon us.

God our helper, defend those who enforce our laws. Bless all police officers to strive for justice and peace. Bless all those who work to protect our city and communities.
Silence
Hear, O Lord;
Have mercy upon us.

God, the restorer of health, hear the prayers of those who cry out to you. Turn their wailing into dancing; clothe them with joy instead of sackcloth.
Invite the congregation to add their petitions and thanksgivings, followed by silence
Hear, O Lord;
Have mercy upon us.

O God, giver of life, you do not abandon your people to the grave. Assure us with the hope of resurrection and your promise of favor forevermore.
Silence
Hear, O Lord;
Have mercy upon us.

Friends, in Christ every one of God's promises is a "Yes." And so we pray to our God, our trustworthy God, saying: "Merciful Lord, *be gracious to us.*"

You, O God, have established your people in your Christ. You have anointed us, put your seal on us, and you have blessed us with your Holy Spirit that we might walk in your ways and live in your truth.
Invite the congregation to add their thanksgivings, followed by silence
Merciful Lord,
Be gracious to us.

Uphold, O Righteous God, those who walk in integrity. Give them the strength to stand for truth in the face of dishonesty. Set the true-of-heart in your presence forever.
Silence
Merciful Lord,
Be gracious to us.

We implore you, O God: do a new thing in our world. Give water in the wilderness; split the desert places with rivers of life. To your people, to those who thirst, give drink, give refreshment.
Silence
Merciful Lord,
Be gracious to us.

Compassionate One, you make happy those who consider the poor. Open our eyes to the poverty in our community and then open our hearts to work for a better, for a more dignified, world.
Silence
Merciful Lord,
Be gracious to us.

Great Healer, we pray for those on their sickbed. In their illness we ask you to heal all their infirmities. Be gracious. Be gracious, Merciful Lord.
Invite the congregation to add their petitions, followed by silence
Merciful Lord,
Be gracious to us.

Blessed are you, Lord God, from everlasting to everlasting. In your presence is true joy. We pray for those who have died. May they dwell with you in everlasting life.
Silence
Merciful Lord,
Be gracious to us.

As far as the east is from the west, so far does God remove from us our transgressions. Let us boldly make our prayer to God, saying: "Bless the Lord, *O my soul!*"

We thank you, O Lord, because you came to call sinners to your side. We are sinners of your own redeeming and you have called us. Thank you, Jesus.
Invite the congregation to add their thanksgivings, followed by silence
Bless the Lord,
O my soul!

Holy God, you work vindication and justice for all who are oppressed. Make us, we pray, a nation that strives for equality, that cares for the lowly.
Silence
Bless the Lord,
O my soul!

We long, O God, for you to make all things right. Let us see the day when you abolish the bow, the sword, and war from the land. Grant us peace and safety.
Silence
Bless the Lord,
O my soul!

Through us, O God, be known in this city. Reveal yourself in your righteousness, and in your justice, in steadfast love, and in mercy.
Silence
Bless the Lord,
O my soul!

Merciful God, you are gracious, slow to anger and abounding in steadfast love. Remind us of your great benefits: heal the diseased and renew the exhausted.
Invite the congregation to add their petitions, followed by silence
Bless the Lord,
O my soul!

Great is your steadfast love, O God. You redeem life from the grave and crown your saints with love and mercy. Grant that those who love you might also reign with you forever.
Silence
Bless the Lord,
O my soul!

God will come and will not keep silence. So let us pray: "Open our eyes; *open our ears."*

Rabbi, it is good for us to be here in your presence. Open our eyes to your glory. Open our ears to your call. Open our lips and our mouths shall proclaim your praise.
Invite the congregation to add their thanksgivings, followed by silence
Open our eyes;
Open our ears.

To those who do not know your love and mercy, reveal yourself, great God. Shine your light through us that our lives might witness to your Son Jesus.
Silence
Open our eyes;
Open our ears.

Holy One, you have chosen to wear the clouds and meet our forebears on the mountains. In doing so, you remind us that you created all things good and continue to manifest your glory through those things you have created. Remind us to also honor your creation.
Silence
Open our eyes;
Open our ears.

O God, we thank you for those women and men in our lives who parent us, teach us, mentor us. Raise up strong leaders, O God, leaders who follow in the footsteps of Jesus.
Silence
Open our eyes;
Open our ears.

You are a powerful God—ruler of the heavens and the earth—and yet, you are close enough to hear our humble prayers. Attend to our loved ones, those we name now.
Invite the congregation to add their petitions, followed by silence
Open our eyes;
Open our ears.

God, you are our hope. Trusting in your goodness, we make our song even at the grave: alleluia, alleluia, alleluia!
Silence
Open our eyes;
Open our ears.

Brothers and sisters, Christ suffered for sins once for all, the righteous for the unrighteous, in order to bring us to God. Let us pray to the God of our salvation, saying, "Show us your ways, O God, *and teach us your paths.*"

You, O God, have saved us through the cleansing waters of baptism. And you have called us to minister in the name of your Son. Send us out today to proclaim the good news of the Kingdom of God.
Silence
Show us your ways, O God,
And teach us your paths.

Let the treacherous be disappointed in their schemes, Righteous God. Deliver the vulnerable from those who would seek to exploit them. Work through us to bring about a just and peaceful world.
Silence
Show us your ways, O God,
And teach us your paths.

Almighty God, you have made a covenant of peace with every living creature that is on the earth. Make us mindful of those creatures with whom we share this planet. May we live in this world with greater respect for everything around us.
Invite the congregation to add their thanksgivings, followed by silence
Show us your ways, O God,
And teach us your paths.

O Lord, defend those who are assailed by any variety of temptation. Give them strength in their weakness. Let none who look to you be put to shame.
Silence
Show us your ways, O God,
And teach us your paths.

Remember, O Lord, your compassion and love. In your mercy, send your healing grace to those in need.
Invite the congregation to add their petitions, followed by silence
Show us your ways, O God,
And teach us your paths.

Jesus Christ, all authorities and powers are subject to you, even the power of death. We pray for those who have died, even as we look in hope to the day of resurrection.
Silence
Show us your ways, O God,
And teach us your paths.

Give praise all you who fear the Lord: proclaim God's greatness! With thankful hearts, let us pray, "O Righteous God, *increase our faith.*"

Lord Jesus, you invite us to follow you: Give your Church the courage and will to risk any and everything for the sake of the gospel. May we be bold in witness and resolute in discipleship.
Silence
O Righteous God,
Increase our faith.

God the King, you rule over the nations: hear the cries of those living in poverty. Give the leaders of nations a heart for the poor.
Silence
O Righteous God,
Increase our faith.

God of Sarah, you bring life out of barren places: renew the creation. Forgive us for our misuse and neglect of your gifts. Help us to live as good stewards.
Silence
O Righteous God,
Increase our faith.

O God, whose glory it is always to have mercy: be gracious to the Church in this city. Strengthen your parishes as we make our Lenten journey. May we faithfully make known your saving deeds.
Invite the congregation to add their thanksgivings, followed by silence
O Righteous God,
Increase our faith.

Gracious Lord, you hide not your face from those in need: we trust in your faithfulness. Hear our prayers for those in pain and distress:
Invite the congregation to add their petitions, followed by silence
O Righteous God,
Increase our faith.

Everliving God, you give life to the dead and call into existence the things that do not exist: hoping against hope, we trust in your eternal promises and look for the day of resurrection.
Silence
O Righteous God,
Increase our faith.

God's foolishness is wiser than human wisdom, and God's weakness is stronger than human strength. Therefore, let us pray to the Lord, saying, "O Lord, our strength and our redeemer, *hear our prayer.*"

Almighty God, you are most fully present, not in any building, but in your Son Jesus: give us the wisdom and strength to remove any obstacles that prevent your people from experiencing your presence.
Silence
O Lord, our strength and our redeemer,
Hear our prayer.

Righteous God, your statutes are just and rejoice the heart: may your justice revive weary souls around the world. We long for the day when your perfect law is valued more than fine gold.
Silence
O Lord, our strength and our redeemer,
Hear our prayer.

Creator God, the heavens declare your glory: train our ears to hear and value the testimony of your handiwork.
Silence
O Lord, our strength and our redeemer,
Hear our prayer.

O Lord, you give wisdom to the innocent: we thank you for libraries and schools and other oases of learning. We thank you for those places where all people, rich and poor, young and old, can increase in knowledge of you and of all you have made.
Invite the congregation to add their thanksgivings, followed by silence
O Lord, our strength and our redeemer,
Hear our prayer.

Gracious God, your steadfast love extends to the thousandth generation of those who love you: we pray that you will defend us, and all whom we love, from all adversities which may happen to the body, and from all evil thoughts which may assault and hurt the soul.
Invite the congregation to add their petitions, followed by silence
O Lord, our strength and our redeemer,
Hear our prayer.

Everliving God, you raised Jesus from the dead: we entrust the dead to the Crucified One in the hope that those who have died in Christ will also be raised to new life in him.
Silence
O Lord, our strength and our redeemer,
Hear our prayer.

God, who is rich in mercy, makes us alive together with Christ. Let us pray to God, saying, "Give thanks to the Lord, for the Lord is good. *Your mercy, O God, endures forever.*"

Holy God, you have created us in Christ Jesus for good works: may the Church walk in the light of Christ, that all our deeds might be good and true and to your glory.
Silence
Give thanks to the Lord, for the Lord is good.
Your mercy, O God, endures forever.

Loving God, you did not send your Son into the world to condemn the world, but in order that the world might be saved through him: may all people know and experience your love.
Silence
Give thanks to the Lord, for the Lord is good.
Your mercy, O God, endures forever.

Jesus, you are the true bread which gives life to the world: feed the world with bread from earth and heaven.
Silence
Give thanks to the Lord, for the Lord is good.
Your mercy, O God, endures forever.

O Lord, you are the deliverer of those in distress: Guide our elected officials. Teach them wisdom and kindness. May they, like Nicodemus, seek to follow in the ways of Jesus.
Silence
Give thanks to the Lord, for the Lord is good.
Your mercy, O God, endures forever.

Merciful God, you send forth your word and the distressed are healed: we give you thanks for your mercy and for the wonders you do for your children.
Invite the congregation to add their petitions and thanksgivings, followed by silence
Give thanks to the Lord, for the Lord is good,
Your mercy, O God, endures forever.

O God, you loved the world so much that you gave your only Son, that eternal life might triumph over death: save us by your grace and raise us up with Christ Jesus.
Silence
Give thanks to the Lord, for the Lord is good,
Your mercy, O God, endures forever.

Jesus said, "Those who love their life lose it, and those who hate their life in this world will keep it for eternal life." So let us appeal to God, saying, "Create in me a clean heart, O God, *and renew a right spirit within me."*

O God, renew your Church: strengthen us to keep the covenant with which you have blessed us. Write your law on our hearts. Be our God and we shall be your beloved people.
Invite the congregation to add their thanksgivings, followed by silence
Create in me a clean heart, O God,
And renew a right spirit within me.

O God, renew all humanity: draw all people to your Son Jesus. May all tribes and nations experience the joy of your saving help.
Silence
Create in me a clean heart, O God,
And renew a right spirit within me.

O God, renew your creation: sustain all you have made with your bountiful Spirit. Reveal your glory in your creation.
Silence
Create in me a clean heart, O God,
And renew a right spirit within me.

O God, renew those wearied by a lack of employment: make them again hear of joy and gladness. Among the swift and varied changes of the world, may they find in you a sure foundation.
Silence
Create in me a clean heart, O God,
And renew a right spirit within me.

O God, renew the sick and sorrowful: have mercy upon them, O God, according to your loving-kindness. Wash them clean, and they shall be clean indeed.
Invite the congregation to add their petitions, followed by silence
Create in me a clean heart, O God,
And renew a right spirit within me.

O God, you make all things new: we thank you that your Son Jesus has become the eternal source of our salvation. Raise those who have died in the flesh to new and everlasting life in Christ.
Silence
Create in me a clean heart, O God,
And renew a right spirit within me.

Though willing in spirit, we are still weak in the flesh. So let us appeal to God's mercy, saying, "Help us, O Lord. *Lord, have mercy.*"

O Lord, let the same mind be in your Church that was in Christ Jesus. With bended knees and confessing tongues, make us able to live his way of humility and obedience.
Silence
Help us, O Lord.
Lord, have mercy.

Almighty God, in your tender love you sent your Son our Savior Jesus to take upon him our human nature, and to suffer death upon the cross, giving us the example of his great humility: give us hearts also to love every human being.
Invite the congregation to add their thanksgivings, followed by silence
Help us, O Lord.
Lord, have mercy.

O God, bless the trees: In celebration of your Son we waved their branches; in our sinful violence we took what you made good and crafted a wooden cross. O God, bless the trees.
Silence
Help us, O Lord.
Lord, have mercy.

Merciful God, look upon our beautiful city. Forgive us our violent ways. Even in hard times, let us not become a reproach to our neighbors. Make your face to shine upon the city.
Silence
Help us, O Lord.
Lord, have mercy.

O Lord, we pray for those who are wasted by grief, whose years are filled with sighing. We pray for those whose strength has failed and whose bones are consumed. In your loving-kindness save them.
Invite the congregation to add their petitions, followed by silence
Help us, O Lord.
Lord, have mercy.

Lord Jesus, you took human form; you died on the cross. You shared with us life and death. We trust the dead to your care. We trust our lives to you.
Silence
Help us, O Lord.
Lord, have mercy.

Easter Day B

Jesus Christ is risen today, our triumphant holy day. Alleluia! So let us pray to our Lord, saying, "Risen Christ, *to you we give undying praise."*

Heavenly King, for us you endured the cross and the grave. When we were yet sinners, you redeemed and saved us. May we sing your eternal praises everywhere we go.
Silence
Risen Christ,
To you we give undying praise.

Paschal victim, where your blood is poured, death's dark angel sheathes his sword. Placing our hope in you, we pray for an end to violence and war.
Silence
Risen Christ,
To you we give undying praise.

Author of Life, you are the ruler of creation. All things created on earth sing to your glory. From the death of the winter, raise the fair beauty of earth.
Silence
Risen Christ,
To you we give undying praise.

Resurrected One, bring our neighbors from sadness into joy. Where they live in darkness, brighten their lives with your splendor and give to all that peace that passes human knowing.
Silence
Risen Christ,
To you we give undying praise.

Jesus the health of the world, pour out your balm on our souls and the souls of all in pain or sorrow. Be the source of life for all people.
Invite the congregation to add their petitions and thanksgivings, followed by silence
Risen Christ,
To you we give undying praise.

Living Christ, nothing in this world can sever us from your love. May we follow where you have gone before us: to rest and reign with you in heaven. Bless and keep the dying and the dead.
Silence
Risen Christ,
To you we give undying praise.

Brothers and sisters, peace be with you. Let us pray to our merciful Lord, saying, "Our Lord and our God, *have mercy on us.*"

Lord Jesus Christ, you have given your Church the gift of your Holy Spirit. May that same Spirit comfort and strengthen us as we proclaim your resurrection to the world.
Silence
Our Lord and our God,
Have mercy on us.

God of wisdom, teach and counsel the leaders of the nations. Fill this world, O God, with justice and peace.
Silence
Our Lord and our God,
Have mercy on us.

God our provider, you have given us this pleasant earth as a goodly heritage. May we use its resources wisely and always according to your purpose.
Invite the congregation to add their thanksgivings, followed by silence
Our Lord and our God,
Have mercy on us.

Righteous God, you are pleased when we live together in unity: may the people of this region be at peace with one another. May our work be rewarding and our needs be met.
Silence
Our Lord and our God,
Have mercy on us.

Merciful God, you are a strong refuge for those in trouble. Protect all those who suffer various trials. Reveal yourself to those for whom faith is a struggle. Make all your people glad by the living hope that is found in you.
Invite the congregation to add their petitions, followed by silence
Our Lord and our God,
Have mercy on us.

God of life, may the dying and the dead rest in hope. Give us faith that you do not abandon anyone, even to the grave. Preserve us for the great inheritance you give us through the resurrection of your Son from the dead.
Silence
Our Lord and our God,
Have mercy on us.

Easter 3B

See what love the Father has given us, that we should be called children of God; and that is what we are. So let us appeal to the Lord, saying, "Answer us when we call, O God; *have mercy on us and hear our prayer.*"

Speak peace to your Church, Lord Christ. Open our minds to your truth. Open our hearts to your presence. Send us forth into the world as witnesses to your resurrection.
Silence
Answer us when we call, O Lord;
Have mercy on us and hear our prayer.

Speak peace to our world, Lord Christ. Many are saying, "Oh, that we might see better times!" Lift up the light of your countenance; give the people of the world hope.
Invite the congregation to add their thanksgivings, followed by silence
Answer us when we call, O Lord;
Have mercy on us and hear our prayer.

Speak peace to the earth, Lord Christ. You entered into the created order and blessed it. Give us eyes to see signs of redemption. Give us courage to responsibly care for all that you have made.
Silence
Answer us when we call, O Lord;
Have mercy on us and hear our prayer.

Speak peace to those who work for the end of hunger and poverty, Lord Christ. You know the pangs of hunger; you know also the depth of our community's need. Comfort and encourage those who become discouraged in their work. Set free all those who are hard-pressed; fulfill all those in need.
Silence
Answer us when we call, O Lord;
Have mercy on us and hear our prayer.

Speak peace to the sick and sorrowful, Lord Christ. When we call upon you, you hear us. You do wonders for the faithful. In your name we pray that our loved ones would have their health restored.
Invite the congregation to add their petitions, followed by silence
Answer us when we call, O Lord;
Have mercy on us and hear our prayer.

Speak peace to those who are dying and those who are grieving, Lord Christ. Having been baptized into your death, O Christ, we await the day when we will be like you, experiencing the fullness of your resurrection.
Silence
Answer us when we call, O Lord;
Have mercy on us and hear our prayer.

Jesus, you are the good shepherd of your people. Hear the cry of your flock as we pray, "Good Shepherd, *receive our prayer.*"

Good Shepherd, you call us to follow where you lead. Give us ears to hear and know your voice. Give us the courage and strength to lay down our lives for one another, as even you laid down your life for us.
Silence
Good Shepherd,
Receive our prayer.

Good Shepherd, gather to yourself the people of the world so there will be one flock under your reign. Forgive us for our hatred and divisions.
Silence
Good Shepherd,
Receive our prayer.

Good Shepherd, you have blessed us with green pastures and still waters—places in your world where we find rest and renewal. We thank you for the beauty of the earth.
Invite the congregation to add their thanksgivings, followed by silence
Good Shepherd,
Receive our prayer.

Good Shepherd, even when wolves attack, you never leave your loved ones; even in the valley of the shadow of death, you are present. Be with all victims of violence. Comfort them in their distress.
Silence
Good Shepherd,
Receive our prayer.

Good Shepherd, you love us so much that you call us each by name: we pray for the healing of our brothers and sisters in your name.
Invite the congregation to add their petitions, followed by silence
Good Shepherd,
Receive our prayer.

Good Shepherd, you are our salvation. Grant all who have died a dwelling place in your house forever.
Silence
Good Shepherd,
Receive our prayer.

Easter 5B

Friends, there is no fear in love, but perfect love casts out fear. So let us boldly pray to God, saying, "Loving God, *put your words in our hearts.*"

Great vine-grower, remove anything in your Church that hinders our love. May we abide in your Son Jesus. May he abide in us. We want to bear much fruit; we want to be disciples of your Son.
Silence
Loving God,
Put your words in our hearts.

Ruler of the nations, under your reign the poor shall eat and be satisfied: make known your saving deeds to the ends of the earth.
Silence
Loving God,
Put your words in our hearts.

Creator God, you nourish our bodies and our spirits with the fruits of the vine. Give us eyes to see your presence in our world; give us words to witness to your goodness.
Invite the congregation to add their thanksgivings, followed by silence
Loving God,
Put your words in our hearts.

Good Teacher, you sent Philip to the Ethiopian so that he would be transformed by understanding: bless our local colleges and universities. Give wisdom and understanding to all those who teach and all those who learn.
Silence
Loving God,
Put your words in our hearts.

O God, you are love. You love us so much. We pray for our brothers and sisters, especially those in great need. Increase our love for them; teach us empathy. Bless them with your healing touch.
Invite the congregation to add their petitions, followed by silence
Loving God,
Put your words in our hearts.

Almighty God, who truly to know is everlasting life: May your love be an eternal abode for all your saints.
Silence
Loving God,
Put your words in our hearts.

The Lord has done marvelous things. So let us boldly pray, saying, "We lift up our voices to you: *Holy Spirit, fall upon us.*"

Loving Parent, you have chosen us to be members of your Church: help us to obey what you command; help us to love one another as you love us.
Silence
We lift up our voices to you:
Holy Spirit, fall upon us.

Loving Parent, you have openly shown your righteousness in the sight of the nations: we pray you judge the people of the world according to your righteousness, not according to our ignorance or folly.
Silence
We lift up our voices to you:
Holy Spirit, fall upon us.

Loving Parent, the rivers clap their hands and the hills ring out with joy before you: open our eyes to recognize your gracious hand in all your works.
Invite the congregation to add their thanksgivings, followed by silence
We lift up our voices to you:
Holy Spirit, fall upon us.

Loving Parent, Jesus taught us that no one has greater love than this, to lay down one's life for one's friends: bless the first responders who consistently risk their health and lives for friends and strangers.
Silence
We lift up our voices to you:
Holy Spirit, fall upon us.

Loving Parent, you always remember your mercy and faithfulness to your people: we ask you, in Jesus' name, to heal and comfort those for whom we pray at this time.
Invite the congregation to add their petitions, followed by silence
We lift up our voices to you:
Holy Spirit, fall upon us.

Loving Parent, you have prepared for those who love you such good things as surpass our understanding: may we, with those who have died, abide in your love forever.
Silence
We lift up our voices to you:
Holy Spirit, fall upon us.

Friends, happy are they who have not walked in the counsel of the wicked. Forgiven and sanctified, let us pray, "Lord, you know everyone's heart. *Show us your will.*"

Christ Jesus, your prayer for your Church is that we may be one as you and the Father are one: sanctify us in your Truth and send us into the world as witnesses to your resurrection.
Silence
Lord, you know everyone's heart.
Show us your will.

O Lord, you know the way of the righteous: rescue and correct all those who walk in the ways of the wicked. Delight the hearts of your children with your perfect law.
Silence
Lord, you know everyone's heart.
Show us your will.

Creator God, bless the fruit-bearing trees; bless the streams. Give us eyes to see clearly the wonders of your universe.
Invite the congregation to add their thanksgivings, followed by silence
Lord, you know everyone's heart.
Show us your will.

Loving Jesus, you guard and protect your own: bless those who, following in your ways, protect and care for society's most vulnerable members, especially children.
Silence
Lord, you know everyone's heart.
Show us your will.

King of Glory, do not leave us comfortless, but send us your Holy Spirit to strengthen us: Comfort and heal all those in peril or need.
Invite the congregation to add their petitions, followed by silence
Lord, you know everyone's heart.
Show us your will.

O God, you have given us eternal life and this life is in your Son, Jesus: may we, with those who have died, enjoy our life with you now and forever.
Silence
Lord, you know everyone's heart.
Show us your will.

Brothers and sisters, we do not know how to pray as we ought, but the Holy Spirit intercedes with sighs too deep for words. So let us make our invocation, "Come, Holy Spirit. *Come, Holy Spirit.*"

Holy God, pour out your Spirit upon your Church. May our young people see visions; may our old people dream dreams. Bless all your ministers, lay and ordained, to declare your salvation.
Silence
Come, Holy Spirit.
Come, Holy Spirit.

Holy God, pour out your Spirit upon all flesh. May young people see visions; may old people dream dreams. May all people experience your salvation.
Silence
Come, Holy Spirit.
Come, Holy Spirit.

Holy God, the whole creation groans for your redemption. You have filled the earth with good things; we often fail to appreciate those good things. Give us eyes to see your saving works in the world around us.
Invite the congregation to add their thanksgivings, followed by silence
Come, Holy Spirit.
Come, Holy Spirit.

Holy God, we thank you for the rich and diverse religious community of our city. We agree and we disagree. Give us faith to trust you to guide all religious communities into all the truth.
Silence
Come, Holy Spirit.
Come, Holy Spirit.

Holy God, grant that all those who are sick and suffering, threatened and afraid, may evermore rejoice in the Spirit's holy comfort.
Invite the congregation to add their petitions, followed by silence
Come, Holy Spirit.
Come, Holy Spirit.

Holy God, you send forth your Spirit to create and renew. Give us patience to hope for that great and glorious day on which the dead shall be raised to new life in your Son Jesus.
Silence
Come, Holy Spirit.
Come, Holy Spirit.

God loved the world so much that God gave the Christ for our salvation. As beloved children of God, let us pray, saying, "Holy, holy, holy, Lord of hosts: *the whole earth is full of your glory.*"

Triune God, you have adopted us as your children and made us joint heirs with Christ: may your church share in Christ's suffering and glory, his death and new life.
Silence
Holy, holy, holy, Lord of hosts:
The whole earth is full of your glory.

Triune God, in Jesus you came into the world not to condemn but to save: may the lonely and condemned experience the depth of your limitless love.
Silence
Holy, holy, holy, Lord of hosts:
The whole earth is full of your glory.

Triune God, we have been born of water, carried on the wind, and made of dust: give us eyes to see our connectedness to all you have created.
Silence
Holy, holy, holy, Lord of hosts:
The whole earth is full of your glory.

Triune God, you have blessed us with this sacred community we call [name of church]: Give us a vision for the future. Send us into the world to share the love we experience in this place.
Invite the congregation to add their thanksgivings, followed by silence
Holy, holy, holy, Lord of hosts:
The whole earth is full of your glory.

Triune God, you are a God of healing: We name in your presence all those who are sick and hurting, the struggling and needy who are known to us.
Invite the congregation to add their petitions, followed by silence
Holy, holy, holy, Lord of hosts:
The whole earth is full of your glory.

Triune God, you offer us eternal life through Jesus: we pray for our dead. Bring us at last, with all those who have died, to see you in your one and eternal glory.
Silence
Holy, holy, holy, Lord of hosts:
The whole earth is full of your glory.

Brothers and sisters, shout for joy to God our strength! Let us avail ourselves to the Ancient of Days, praying, "We are open to you, O God; *fill us with your Spirit.*"

Give us the strength to keep a holy Sabbath. As the world bustles and produces and consumes, make us a people of prayer, and rest, and holy fellowship.
Silence
We are open to you, O God;
Fill us with your Spirit.

Remind us, O God, of your faithfulness to our ancestors. You have been our help in ages past. You have showed us compassion; may we be compassionate also to others.
Invite the congregation to add thanksgivings, followed by silence
We are open to you, O God;
Fill us with your Spirit.

You have blessed us with the gift of rest, O God. May we, especially when we hold positions of authority, not withhold rest from others. In our drive to be productive, may we not forget to bless the earth with rest as well.
Silence
We are open to you, O God;
Fill us with your Spirit.

Make us a light in our community. May the lost and those who sit in darkness see in us the light and life of Jesus.
Silence
We are open to you, O God;
Fill us with your Spirit.

Lord Jesus, you delight in making us well. You delight in doing good. You delight in life—abundant life. You bring to yourself those who are suffering, those who are distressed, and those in need.
Invite the congregation to add their petitions, followed by silence
We are open to you, O God;
Fill us with your Spirit.

We carry in our bodies, O Lord, the death of your Son. And as we share in his death, raise us and all who die in the Lord to newness of life.
Silence
We are open to you, O God;
Fill us with your Spirit.

Brothers and sisters, when we call, the Lord answers us. Knowing that our prayers are heard by our great God, let us make our appeal, "O Lord, we are members of your family; *make good your purpose for us.*"

We call to you, O Lord: Hear our prayers for the Church. Give us discerning eyes to see the work of your Spirit in our lives. Guard our hearts that we might not take for granted our place in your family.
Silence
O Lord, we are members of your family;
Make good your purpose for us.

We call to you, O Lord: hear our prayers for the world. Though you are high, you care for the lowly. May the kings and rulers of the world look to you, O God, for wisdom and guidance.
Silence
O Lord, we are members of your family;
Make good your purpose for us.

We call to you, O Lord: hear our prayers for all creation. Do not abandon the works of your hands. Bless and preserve all that you have made.
Silence
O Lord, we are members of your family;
Make good your purpose for us.

We call to you, O Lord: hear our prayers for those people who create and those institutions that preserve all things artistic. From you proceeds all good and beautiful things. We thank you that you inspire men and women to create. We thank you that you are known to us in many and diverse ways.
Invite the congregation to add their thanksgivings, followed by silence
O Lord, we are members of your family;
Make good your purpose for us.

We call to you, O Lord: hear our prayers for those in need. It is you who increases strength in the weak, who keeps safe those in the midst of trouble. By your right hand, offer your saving help.
Invite the congregation to add their petitions, followed by silence
O Lord, we are members of your family;
Make good your purpose for us.

We call to you, O Lord: hear our prayers for the dying and the dead. Even as our outer nature is wasting away, you daily renew our spirits. We trust that, as you raised Jesus from the dead, so will you raise us with him and bring us into your loving presence forever.
Silence
O Lord, we are members of your family;
Make good your purpose for us.

Brothers and sisters, we walk by faith, not by sight. Trusting that God hears our prayers, let us cry to the Lord, saying, "We call upon your Name, O Lord! *Answer us when we call.*"

We call to you, O Lord: hear our prayers for the Church. Keep us steadfast in faith and love, that we may proclaim your truth with boldness and minister your justice with compassion.
Silence
We call upon your Name, O Lord!
Answer us when we call.

We call to you, O Lord: hear our prayers for the world. For love, your Son Jesus died for all. We pray that all the people of the world come to know that love.
Silence
We call upon your Name, O Lord!
Answer us when we call.

We call to you, O Lord: hear our prayers for all creation. Bless seeds to produce. Bless fields to yield their crop. Bless those who plant and those who gather. May all be blessed by the harvest.
Silence
We call upon your Name, O Lord!
Answer us when we call.

We call to you, O Lord: hear our prayers for all artists, poets, dancers and musicians. Remember their offerings of beauty and inspiration and prosper their plans. We thank you for the blessed gift of creativity.
Invite the congregation to add their thanksgivings, followed by silence
We call upon your Name, O Lord!
Answer us when we call.

We call to you, O Lord: hear our prayers for those in need. Answer them in their day of trouble. Send them help and strengthen them to stand.
Invite the congregation to add their petitions, followed by silence
We call upon your Name, O Lord!
Answer us when we call.

We call to you, O Lord: hear our prayers for the dying and the dead. Raise those who have died in the body to newness of life. Grant them a home with you forever.
Silence
We call upon your Name, O Lord!
Answer us when we call.

Proper 7B

Brothers and sisters, may the Lord be with you! Trusting that our God listens when we pray, let us say, "We put our trust in you, O Lord. *Answer with your peace.*"

We call to you, O Lord: hear our prayers for the Church. Set us upon the sure foundation of your loving-kindness. Open wide our hearts to accept your grace.
Invite the congregation to add their thanksgivings, followed by silence
We put our trust in you, O Lord.
Answer with your peace.

We call to you, O Lord: hear our prayers for the world. You are known by your acts of justice. Let the hope of the poor be not taken away.
Silence
We put our trust in you, O Lord.
Answer with your peace.

We call to you, O Lord: hear our prayers for all creation. Even the wind and the sea obey your command. Speak peace and life to all you have made.
Silence
We put our trust in you, O Lord.
Answer with your peace.

We call to you, O Lord: hear our prayers for those who live without a place to call home. You are a refuge for the oppressed, a shelter in time of trouble. Do not forsake those who seek your help.
Silence
We put our trust in you, O Lord.
Answer with your peace.

We call to you, O Lord: hear our prayers for those in any kind of need. You do not forget the needy; they are ever in your thoughts. You hear the cry of the afflicted. Fill down-turned mouths with songs of praise and rejoicing.
Invite the congregation to add their petitions, followed by silence
We put our trust in you, O Lord.
Answer with your peace.

We call to you, O Lord: hear our prayers for the dying and the dead. You are the God of life; you lift your people from the gates of death. We commend to your mercy all who have died.
Silence
We put our trust in you, O Lord.
Answer with your peace.

Brothers and sisters, wait for the Lord, for with the Lord there is mercy. Let us appeal to God's mercy, praying, "Consider well the voice of our supplication; *Lord, hear our voice.*"

Out of the depths we call to you, O Lord, for the Church. Be present with those who take counsel for the renewal and mission of your Church. Guide the Church into all truth and goodness. May all we do witness to your love.
Silence
Consider well the voice of our supplication;
Lord, hear our voice.

Out of the depths we call to you, O Lord, for the world. We pray for all those who wait in hope for you. Let them not be disappointed.
Silence
Consider well the voice of our supplication;
Lord, hear our voice.

Out of the depths we call to you, O Lord, for all creation. In the hour of our abundance may we be generous; in our hour of need may we find relief.
Invite the congregation to add their thanksgivings, followed by silence
Consider well the voice of our supplication;
Lord, hear our voice.

Out of the depths we call to you, O Lord, for the city of [_____]. Bless our city. May it be rich in knowledge and generosity. May it never be said of us, "How the mighty have fallen."
Silence
Consider well the voice of our supplication;
Lord, hear our voice.

Out of the depths we call to you, O Lord, for those who suffer afflictions of many kinds. Lord Christ, be the healer of broken bodies, broken lives and broken hearts.
Invite the congregation to add their petitions, followed by silence
Consider well the voice of our supplication;
Lord, hear our voice.

Out of the depths we call to you, O Lord, for all who have died in the hope of the resurrection. Even as we lament the death of those we love, we trust in your victory over the grave; we trust in the strength of your love.
Silence
Consider well the voice of our supplication;
Lord, hear our voice.

Great is the Lord, and highly to be praised! Let us offer our prayers, saying, "Be our guide, O God, for evermore: *send us out to do the work you have given us to do.*"

O God, send us out to proclaim the good news of repentance and forgiveness in Jesus' name. By the sufficiency of your grace, comfort and strengthen your Church. We pray especially for our bishop and our clergy. May all those who take council for the Church be wholly devoted to you.
Silence
Be our guide, O God, forevermore:
Send us out to do the work you have given us to do.

O God, send us out, that your praise might reach to the ends of the earth. May all know your right hand to be full of justice; defend the poor and oppressed.
Silence
Be our guide, O God, forevermore:
Send us out to do the work you have given us to do.

O God, all that you touch is beautiful; your holy presence brings joy to all the earth: bless your creation with prosperity.
Silence
Be our guide, O God, forevermore:
Send us out to do the work you have given us to do.

O God, we thank you for our parks and places of recreation. Bless them to be places of welcome and hospitality. Bless us with opportunities to take pleasure in beauty and leisure.
Invite the congregation to add their thanksgivings, followed by silence
Be our guide, O God, forevermore:
Send us out to do the work you have given us to do.

O God, send us out into the world to pray for and love those in need. Strengthen our faith in your healing power. We pray to you for the sick and suffering today because we trust in your love.
Invite the congregation to add their petitions, followed by silence
Be our guide, O God, forevermore:
Send us out to do the work you have given us to do.

O God, you have established your heavenly kingdom forever. Bring us, with all who have died, into the eternal joy of that kingdom.
Silence
Be our guide, O God, forevermore:
Send us out to do the work you have given us to do.

Friends, we have been chosen by God in Christ to be holy and blameless before God in love! Offer your prayers, saying, "O Lord, mercifully receive the prayers of your people; *Lord, have mercy.*"

We thank you, Lord Christ, that you have redeemed us, that you forgive us our trespasses, that you lavish us with grace. Grant to your church understanding that we may accomplish your purposes.
Silence
Invite the congregation to add their thanksgivings, followed by silence
O Lord, mercifully receive the prayers of your people;
Lord, have mercy.

O God, raise up prophets like your servants John the baptizer and the prophets of old. Give courage and clarity to those who would speak truth to the world's power.
Silence
O Lord, mercifully receive the prayers of your people;
Lord, have mercy.

O Lord, the earth is yours and all that is in it, the world and all who dwell therein. Give us wisdom as we steward what belongs to you; give us the will to care for your creation.
Silence
O Lord, mercifully receive the prayers of your people;
Lord, have mercy.

Just as David employed men to carry the sacred ark, we acknowledge before you our reliance on the efforts of others. Bless those who labor on our behalf and for our benefit. We pray for the day when all workers earn a fair wage.
Silence
O Lord, mercifully receive the prayers of your people;
Lord, have mercy.

Jesus, in your name and by your hand the sick are anointed, the suffering are set free, and the heartbroken are healed. We pray for our sisters and brothers who are in need of your touch.
Invite the congregation to add their petitions, followed by silence
O Lord, mercifully receive the prayers of your people;
Lord, have mercy.

O God, it is your good pleasure, in the fullness of time, to gather all things to yourself. May those who have died enjoy forever the inheritance you have prepared for us in Christ.
Silence
O Lord, mercifully receive the prayers of your people;
Lord, have mercy.

Brothers and sisters, the Lord is with us. The Almighty is compassionate and hears our prayers; so let us pray, "Compassionate Lord, *have mercy on us.*"

Loving God, through the waters of baptism you have accepted us as members of your household; through Christ Jesus you have made us your dwelling place. Have compassion on our weakness; work powerfully through your Church.
Silence
Compassionate Lord,
Have mercy on us.

Lord Jesus, you proclaim peace to those who are far off and those who are near; you make strangers and aliens citizens of your kingdom. We give you thanks for your welcoming, steadfast love.
Silence
Invite the congregation to add their thanksgivings, followed by silence
Compassionate Lord,
Have mercy on us.

Loving God, your covenant with your creation you will never break. Give us the will to live at peace with all you have made.
Silence
Compassionate Lord,
Have mercy on us.

Lord Jesus, you look at the hungry and the poor with compassion. Fill our hearts with the same compassion. Inspire us to love and serve those with whom we share our communities.
Silence
Compassionate Lord,
Have mercy on us.

Lord Jesus, in your presence is healing and strength. We bring to you our sick and suffering.
Invite the congregation to add their petitions, followed by silence
Compassionate Lord,
Have mercy on us.

Loving God, we commend to you the dying and the dead. Bring them we pray into that heavenly country, where with apostles and prophets, they will live forever with Christ Jesus.
Silence
Compassionate Lord,
Have mercy on us.

My sisters and brothers, may Christ dwell in your hearts by faith. Let us pray for the whole state of Christ's Church, saying, "Lord Christ, you are the bread of life; *fill us with your goodness.*"

O Lord, be glorified in your Church. Give us faith to trust in you, that we might ever believe the truth of your word.
Silence
Lord Christ, you are the bread of life;
Fill us with your goodness.

O Lord, look in mercy upon your children. Inspire understanding in those who do not yet seek your ways. Count us, just God, among the generation of the righteous.
Silence
Lord Christ, you are the bread of life;
Fill us with your goodness.

Lord Christ, you tamed the raging of the sea and the strength of the wind. We pray you to shield our crops from the fury of the sun; bless our fields with waters from the heavens.
Silence
Lord Christ, you are the bread of life;
Fill us with your goodness.

O Lord, we hold in our hearts all victims of violence—especially those smitten by gun violence. May they, and those who love them, comprehend with all the saints what is the breadth, and length, and depth, and height of your comforting love.
Silence
Lord Christ, you are the bread of life;
Fill us with your goodness.

Jesus, you said to your disciples, "It is I; be not afraid." We pray you to comfort all who are in trouble, need, or sickness.
Invite the congregation to add their petitions and thanksgivings, followed by silence
Lord Christ, you are the bread of life;
Fill us with your goodness.

O God, you have gathered as your family those on heaven and earth. We pray for those who have died that they may rest in your eternal presence. And we pray for ourselves that we may run the race with vigor and finally join your saints forever.
Silence
Lord Christ, you are the bread of life;
Fill us with your goodness.

Brothers and sisters, bear with one another in love. And cry out to God in one voice: "Create in me a clean heart, O God, *and renew a right spirit within me."*

Loving God, you have blessed us with all we need to do the work to which we have been called. Bless those in our midst who are gifted to be apostles, prophets, evangelists, pastors, and teachers. Build up the body of Christ.
Silence
Create in me a clean heart, O God,
and renew a right spirit within me.

Bless the hungry with good things, Generous God. Sustain our bodies and our souls. Show yourself to be the God who provides for the needy and cares for the poor.
Silence
Create in me a clean heart, O God,
and renew a right spirit within me.

You are good to us, O God. We thank you for this planet. We thank you that you continue to cause new life to grow and thrive.
Invite the congregation to add their thanksgivings, followed by silence
Create in me a clean heart, O God,
and renew a right spirit within me.

Fill our communities with humility and gentleness. We pray, O God, that neighbors might live together in love and respect. Give us the grace to build peaceful neighborhoods, peaceful cities, peaceful nations, and a peaceful world.
Silence
Create in me a clean heart, O God,
and renew a right spirit within me.

When we are frustrated and scared, when we are desperate and in need, you, Loving God, hear our prayers. Hear them again today.
Invite the congregation to add their petitions, followed by silence
Create in me a clean heart, O God,
and renew a right spirit within me.

You are a God of mercy; you judge us according to your loving-kindness. Look at us through your eyes of mercy, now and in the hour of our death.
Silence
Create in me a clean heart, O God,
and renew a right spirit within me.

Brothers and sisters, forgive one another as God in Christ has forgiven you.
With purified hearts, let us offer ourselves to God in prayer, saying, "Bread of Life,
we are hungry for you."

O Lord, you have sealed us by the Holy Spirit and marked us as Christ's own
forever: may we live in love with each other, as Christ loves us.
Silence
Bread of Life,
We are hungry for you.

O Lord, we weep with David over the cost of war—the lives lost and destroyed.
We pray for peace and an end to all violence.
Silence
Bread of Life,
We are hungry for you.

O Lord, with you there is plenteous redemption. Restore and recreate the world in
which we live and bless us to live at peace with all things.
Silence
Bread of Life,
We are hungry for you.

O Lord, we give you thanks for all police officers—especially those who serve our
city. Give them grace to labor and work honestly to uphold justice with mercy.
Invite the congregation to add their thanksgivings, followed by silence
Bread of Life,
We are hungry for you.

O Lord, let your ears consider well the voices of the needy. For the sick and hurting
and all those who call to you from the depths, we now pray.
Invite the congregation to add their petitions, followed by silence
Bread of Life,
We are hungry for you.

O Lord, you are the Bread of Life. We thank you for offering your own flesh for the
life of the world. Keep us, and all those who have died, in eternal life.
Silence
Bread of Life,
We are hungry for you.

Brothers and sisters, the fear of the Lord is the beginning of wisdom. Let us offer to God our prayers, saying, "At all times and for all things: *wise God, we give you thanks.*"

Faithful God, you are ever mindful of the covenant you made with your Church in baptism: Give us grace to follow daily in the blessed steps of your Son Jesus.
Silence
At all times and for all things:
Wise God, we give you thanks.

O Lord, for the sake of this nation and for the world, give to our elected officials wise and discerning minds. May all our works be done in truth and equity.
Silence
At all times and for all things:
Wise God, we give you thanks.

Mighty Creator, your work is full of majesty and splendor. Give us the vision to look upon all you have made with awe and wonder and give you thanks.
Invite the congregation to add their thanksgivings, followed by silence
At all times and for all things:
Wise God, we give you thanks.

God, we praise you for children. We pray that our hearts might be humbled to learn from our youngest brothers and sisters what it means to be gracious, compassionate, and filled with the Spirit.
Silence
At all times and for all things:
Wise God, we give you thanks.

Merciful Lord, great are your deeds and marvelous are your works: we pray for those in need of your help and healing, trusting in your righteousness.
Invite the congregation to add their petitions, followed by silence
At all times and for all things:
Wise God, we give you thanks.

Lord Christ, Living Bread, you promise eternal life for all who eat of your body: grant to us, and to all who have died, eternal life in your heavenly kingdom.
Silence
At all times and for all things:
Wise God, we give you thanks.

Brothers and sisters, the scriptures implore us to pray in the Spirit at all times in every prayer and supplication. So let us offer to God our prayers, saying, "Regard your servant's prayer: *hear our plea, O Lord our God."*

O Lord of hosts, happy are they who put their trust in you: behold your Church, O God; defend your children against the wiles of the devil.
Silence
Regard your servant's prayer;
Hear our plea, O Lord our God.

O Lord, you bless with good things those who walk with integrity: behold your world, O God; may your grace and glory shine like the sun over the nations.
Invite the congregation to add their thanksgivings, followed by silence
Regard your servant's prayer;
Hear our plea, O Lord our God.

Mighty Creator, you make a home in your presence for even the littlest sparrow: behold the stewards of creation, O God; may we live at peace with all you have made.
Silence
Regard your servant's prayer;
Hear our plea, O Lord our God.

Strong Lord, in your presence desolate valleys burst forth with springs of water: behold those struggling with addiction; defend and free them from the powers of their present darkness that they may walk in light and clarity all the days of their lives.
Regard your servant's prayer;
Hear our plea, O Lord our God.

Holy One of God, your words are spirit and life: behold those in need of prayer this day; restore all to wholeness and health by your powerful touch.
Invite the congregation to add their petitions, followed by silence
Regard your servant's prayer;
Hear our plea, O Lord our God.

Lord Christ, Living Bread, you offer yourself that we might live forever: in your compassion, look upon the dying and the dead.
Silence
Regard your servant's prayer;
Hear our plea, O Lord our God.

My brothers and sisters, welcome with meekness the word planted within you that has the power to save your souls. In all humility let us pray, saying, "Increase in us true religion; *nourish us with all goodness.*"

Gracious God, you have given us birth by the word of truth: speak lovingly to your beloved Church. Increase in us true religion that we may honor you in both word and deed.
Silence
Increase in us true religion;
Nourish us with all goodness.

Righteous God, you know our hearts: deliver us from our own evil intentions and protect us from the evil intentions of others.
Silence
Increase in us true religion;
Nourish us with all goodness.

Creating God, you are the author and giver of all good things: forgive us when we forget to sing your praises for the beauty of the earth. We thank you for the eternal blossoming of creation.
Invite the congregation to add their thanksgivings, followed by silence
Increase in us true religion;
Nourish us with all goodness.

Gracious God, we thank you for the towns and villages that surround our city. Bless our common life and work. In our dealings may we be quick to listen, slow to speak, and slow to anger. May each community lay aside selfish interests to pursue the common good.
Silence
Increase in us true religion;
Nourish us with all goodness.

Holy Father, with you there is no variation or shadow due to change: Surround those in distress with your healing light. Remove their pain and anoint them with the oil of gladness
Invite the congregation to add their petitions, followed by silence
Increase in us true religion;
Nourish us with all goodness.

Holy God, your throne endures forever and ever: bring us, at last, with all your saints, into your heavenly kingdom.
Silence
Increase in us true religion;
Nourish us with all goodness.

My brothers and sisters, those who trust in the Lord stand fast forever. Relying on our God, let us pray, "Show your goodness, O Lord; *Lord, have mercy.*"

Grant us, O Lord, to trust in you with all our hearts. Deliver your Church from making hurtful distinctions and from all evil thoughts.
Silence
Show your goodness, O Lord;
Lord, have mercy.

Lord God, we pray for the poor. It is you who plead their cause, who defend their dignity. Give us hearts to love others as we are loved by you.
Silence
Show your goodness, O Lord;
Lord, have mercy.

Loving God, maker and creator of all things, we give you thanks for the beauty of creation and for the gifts of the earth.
Invite the congregation to add their thanksgivings, followed by silence
Show your goodness, O Lord;
Lord, have mercy.

We pray for those who work to preserve the lives of your creatures. We thank you, O God, for the amazing diversity with which you have blessed us.
Silence
Show your goodness, O Lord;
Lord, have mercy.

Loving Jesus, in your words, in your touch, is healing. Speak new life to those suffering, to those in need of mercy.
Invite the congregation to add their petitions, followed by silence
Show your goodness, O Lord;
Lord, have mercy.

Gracious God, with you mercy triumphs over judgment. Accept the dead into your great mercy. May we, with all who have died, dwell in your love forever.
Silence
Show your goodness, O Lord;
Lord, have mercy.

My brothers and sisters, those who lose their life for Jesus' sake, and for the sake of the gospel, will save it. Trusting in our God, let us pray, "Spirit, direct our hearts; *Spirit, rule our hearts.*"

Bless your Church, O God, with wisdom. Make our souls holy and grant to us your friendship and love.
Silence
Spirit, direct our hearts;
Spirit, rule our hearts.

O God, inspire a love for wisdom in the leaders of the nations, in the leaders of communities, in the leaders of people. Give us the will to raise up leaders who heed wisdom's cries.
Silence
Spirit, direct our hearts;
Spirit, rule our hearts.

The heavens declare your glory, blessed Creator; the firmament shows your handiwork. Give us ears to hear, eyes to see, and mouths to sing your praises.
Invite the congregations to add their thanksgivings, followed by silence
Spirit, direct our hearts;
Spirit, rule our hearts.

We pray, O God, that you guide and direct those who work in the financial and business sectors. May they desire your righteousness more than much fine gold.
Silence
Spirit, direct our hearts;
Spirit, rule our hearts.

Messiah Jesus, it is you who gives light to the eyes and rejoices the heart. We pray for those in need of your touch. Renew the tired, the sick, and the struggling.
Invite the congregation to add their petitions, followed by silence
Spirit, direct our hearts;
Spirit, rule our hearts.

Lord Christ, you are life and you are salvation. Keep those who have died as your own forever.
Silence
Spirit, direct our hearts;
Spirit, rule our hearts.

Friends, draw near to God, and God will draw near to you. With open and humble hearts, let us pray, saying, "We have asked wrongly before, O Lord; *may this request be righteous."*

Give to your Church, O God, wisdom from above. Let us be known as people of peace, gentleness, and mercy.
Silence
We have asked wrongly before, O Lord;
May this request be righteous.

Lover of souls, we pray for all women and girls around the world. May those who have been oppressed and ignored walk with strength and dignity. We thank you, O God, for women.
Invite the congregation to add their thanksgivings, followed by silence
We have asked wrongly before, O Lord;
May this request be righteous.

O God, we pray for this earth, our island home. May we not be anxious about earthly things, but give us hope that you are refreshing the resources that we have exploited and misused.
Silence
We have asked wrongly before, O Lord;
May this request be righteous.

Heavenly Father, your son was betrayed, arrested, and killed: be with all captives and prisoners. Fill us with your mercy and wisdom. May our lives show forth the way of the righteous.
Silence
We have asked wrongly before, O Lord;
May this request be righteous.

Holy God, we ask you to strengthen and heal our ailing loved ones. Bring forth in them good fruit and prosper all that they do in Jesus' name.
Invite the congregation to add their petitions, followed by silence
We have asked wrongly before, O Lord;
May this request be righteous.

Lord, we pray for those who have died. We thank you for those who have showed us faith and wisdom. May we, following the example of our forebears, hold fast to those things that shall endure.
Silence
We have asked wrongly before, O Lord;
May this request be righteous.

Proper 21B

My brothers and sisters, the prayer of the righteous is powerful and effective. Believing in the power of prayer, let us pray to the Lord, saying, "God our help; *receive our prayer.*"

Give to your Church, O God, the vision to see you at work in the world. Forgive us when we try to limit or control you. May we rejoice in all good and celebrate all loving deeds.
Silence
God our help;
Receive our prayer.

O God, you declare your almighty power chiefly in showing mercy and pity: comfort all those around the globe who know the devastation of war and the threat of annihilation. We pray for peace.
Silence
God our help;
Receive our prayer.

We thank you, O God, that you have provided us with those things that make our lives better—fire for heat, salt for seasoning. We thank you for all of the good gifts we so easily take for granted.
Invite the congregation to add their thanksgivings, followed by silence
God our help;
Receive our prayer.

We pray, O God, for all those with whom we share this city. Bring people together. Enable healthy relationships. Help us to be at peace with one another.
Silence
God our help;
Receive our prayer.

Blessed God, as you command us, we pray for those in need of healing and wholeness. Turn their sorrow into gladness and their mourning into holiday. Lord, raise them up in Jesus' name.
Invite the congregation to add their petitions, followed by silence
God our help;
Receive our prayer.

Almighty God, were you not on our side, we would be without hope. But you are our salvation. Grant us entrance into your heavenly kingdom; may we become partakers of your heavenly treasure.
Silence
God our help;
Receive our prayer.

Sisters and brothers, God has made us for each other. So joining our voices together, let us pray, "O Lord our Governor, *how exalted is your Name in all the world!*"

Heavenly Parent, give to your Church the faith to accept your kingdom as a little child. Bless us with grace and love so that we might love those who share with us your kingdom.
Silence
O Lord our Governor,
How exalted is your Name in all the world!

What are mortals, O Ancient of Days, that you are mindful of us? And yet you are. We praise you for your goodness and your overwhelming compassion.
Invite the congregation to add their thanksgivings, followed by silence
O Lord our Governor,
How exalted is your Name in all the world!

When we consider your heavens, the works of your fingers, the moon and the stars you have set in their courses, we stand in awe. O God, we praise you for all your works.
Silence
O Lord our Governor,
How exalted is your Name in all the world!

We ask your blessing, O God, on all married and partnered couples. You know the challenges committed couples face. You know the temptations and the stressors. But it is your desire that what you have joined, no one separate. So increase our love and understanding.
Silence
O Lord our Governor,
How exalted is your Name in all the world!

Lord Jesus, you sustain all things by your powerful word. Sustain those who are wearied by illness or sorrow. Come, Great Healer, come.
Invite the congregation to add their petitions, followed by silence
O Lord our Governor,
How exalted is your Name in all the world!

By your incredible grace, O God, your Son tasted death for us and by his sufferings perfected our salvation. Grant to those who die a place with your Son, and all the saints, in your eternal kingdom.
Silence
O Lord our Governor,
How exalted is your Name in all the world!

My sisters and brothers, let us approach the throne of grace with boldness, so that we may receive mercy and find grace in time of need. Trusting in God's grace, we pray, "Be not far from us, O God; *for we put our trust in you.*"

Holy God, give us grace to follow Jesus. Fill us where we are found lacking. Purge from us all those things that would cause us to stray from the path Jesus has marked for us.
Silence
Be not far from us, O God;
For we put our trust in you.

Almighty God, we pray for all those who feel forsaken. We pray that you will hear the bitter complaints of the oppressed and forlorn. Answer their cries and be their deliverer.
Silence
Be not far from us, O God;
For we put our trust in you.

Mighty Creator, you are great in power and yet you sympathize with us in our weakness: reveal yourself to us through the vast diversity of creation. We stand in awe of your severity and your delicacy.
Silence
Be not far from us, O God;
For we put our trust in you.

Bless, Great Healer, all doctors, nurses, and all those who work for the wellness of others. May your grace always precede and follow them, that they may be good stewards of their gifts and remember that all life and healing comes from you.
Invite the congregation to add their thanksgivings, followed by silence
Be not far from us, O God;
For we put our trust in you.

Holy One, from birth until even this moment your loving gaze has never faltered. Just as you did for our forebears, heal and deliver those who trust in you.
Invite the congregation to add their petitions, followed by silence
Be not far from us, O God;
For we put our trust in you.

O God, for you all things are possible. Only by your grace are we saved. Grant us, with all those who have followed your Son in ages past, eternal life.
Silence
Be not far from us, O God;
For we put our trust in you.

Jesus said, "Whoever wishes to become great among you must be your servant, and whoever wishes to be first among you must be slave of all." As members of the household of God and fellow servants of Christ, let us pray together, saying, "Bless the Lord, O my soul; *hallelujah!*"

Almighty God, give your Church to works of mercy; give us hearts to serve; give us the courage to follow Jesus.
Silence
Bless the Lord, O 'my soul;
Hallelujah!

Almighty God, in Christ you have revealed your glory among the nations: grant to the peoples of the world peace and freedom.
Silence
Bless the Lord, O my soul;
Hallelujah!

O Lord, how manifold are your works! In wisdom you have made them all; the earth is full of your creatures. We are in awe of your greatness.
Invite the congregation to add their thanksgivings, followed by silence
Bless the Lord, O my soul;
Hallelujah!

Jesus, you call us to service: We thank you for the ministries in our community with which we work closely. We pray you bless them; bless all those who benefit from their generosity; and bless our common mission.
Silence
Bless the Lord, O my soul;
Hallelujah!

Jesus, our great high priest, you know our weakness and our suffering: bless and heal all those in need.
Invite the congregation to add their petitions, followed by silence
Bless the Lord, O my soul;
Hallelujah!

O God, you alone are able to save us from eternal death: grant us, and all those we love but see no longer, eternal salvation through your Son.
Silence
Bless the Lord, O my soul;
Hallelujah!

Jesus, our high priest, always lives to make intercession for us. Let us cry out to the Lord who hears us and prays for us, "We know that you can do all things; *Jesus, have mercy on us!*"

Jesus, pray for your Church: Increase in us the gifts of faith, hope, and charity. Hold us together as one people with one Lord.
Silence
We know that you can do all things;
Jesus, have mercy on us!

Jesus, pray for the world: may all those who live in fear and terror find their deliverance in you.
Silence
We know that you can do all things;
Jesus, have mercy on us!

Jesus, pray for the creation: you are great and all things created through you are good. May we treasure all the gifts from your hand.
Invite the congregation to add their thanksgivings, followed by silence
We know that you can do all things;
Jesus, have mercy on us!

Jesus, pray for those who farm: bless those who toil so that we may have food to eat and clothes to wear. May their needs be met and their work rewarding.
Silence
We know that you can do all things;
Jesus, have mercy on us!

Jesus, pray for those who are sick and struggling: in their affliction hear their cries and save them from all their troubles.
Invite the congregation to add their petitions, followed by silence
We know that you can do all things;
Jesus, have mercy on us!

Jesus, keep the dead in your love forever: by offering yourself you have made us holy. Have mercy on us and bring us to your heavenly country, with all your saints, to worship in your presence forever.
Silence
We know that you can do all things;
Jesus, have mercy on us!

Happy are they who walk in the law of the Lord! Let us seek God with all our hearts, praying, "Direct our ways; *make straight our paths.*"

Lord our God, bind your gospel on our lips, fix it in our minds, and write it on our hearts. May the world see and know that your Church loves you.
Silence
Direct our ways;
Make straight our paths.

You command us to love our neighbors as ourselves. As a nation, teach us to value our neighbors around the world, treating them with dignity and respect. Help us, O God, to keep your commandments.
Silence
Direct our ways;
Make straight our paths.

You command us to love our neighbors as ourselves. Teach us to value our neighbors—in our city, around the corner, and even next door. Help us, O God, to keep your commandments.
Silence
Direct our ways;
Make straight our paths.

You have ordered and established the world in which we live, Creator God. Give us wisdom and grace to honor your creation.
Invite the congregation to add their thanksgivings, followed by silence
Direct our ways;
Make straight our paths.

Do not forsake your beloved ones in their misery. Heal, O God, those in need.
Invite the congregation to add their petitions, followed by silence
Direct our ways;
Make straight our paths.

Almighty God, you offer your children eternal redemption. We commend to your mercy all those who have died.
Silence
Direct our ways;
Make straight our paths.

All Saints' Day B (or the Sunday closest)

The One who is seated on the eternal throne says, "See, I am making all things new."
Let us pray to the only One who makes us worthy, saying, "Cleanse our hands;
purify our hearts!"

God of the saints, give us grace to follow your blessed ones in all virtuous and godly
living. Embolden us to unbind what you are bringing to new life.
Silence
Cleanse our hands;
Purify our hearts!

God of the saints, you are the King of Glory: guide the people of our land. May we
never forget that you alone are our hope and salvation.
Silence
Cleanse our hands;
Purify our hearts!

God of the saints, the earth is yours and all that is in it, the world and all who dwell
therein. May we be respectful of all that you have made.
Silence
Cleanse our hands;
Purify our hearts!

God of the saints, we pray for all those who share in the work of this [diocese]. Knit
us together in one communion and fellowship, and then use us, we pray, to proclaim
your Kingdom within our borders.
Invite the congregation to add their thanksgivings, followed by silence
Cleanse our hands;
Purify our hearts!

God of the saints, we hope for the day when you will wipe away the tears from all
faces. Give us a glimpse of what is to come: heal and comfort those for whom we
pray—especially those who mourn.
Invite the congregation to add their petitions, followed by silence
Cleanse our hands;
Purify our hearts!

God of the saints, we trust our lives and the lives of the dead to you. And we pray
for the day when death will be no more, when mourning and crying and pain will
be no more.
Silence
Cleanse our hands;
Purify our hearts!

Christ appears in the presence of God on our behalf. With such a great advocate, let us pray to God for ourselves and for others, saying, "Blessed are you, O Lord; *you supply all our needs.*"

God of blessing, we wait in hope for you. We wait for your kingdom to come; we wait for the return of your Son; we wait for you to visit us with your Holy Spirit once again today. We wait in hope for you; give us patience.
Silence
Blessed are you, O Lord;
You supply all our needs.

God of blessing, we pray you guide and protect our service men and women. Let those who trust in you never be put to shame.
Invite the congregation to add their thanksgivings, followed by silence
Blessed are you, O Lord;
You supply all our needs.

God of blessing, we pray that you bless the earth to bear much fruit. May there be enough to feed all of the people of the world. May those with much and those with little rejoice together in your bounty.
Silence
Blessed are you, O Lord;
You supply all our needs.

God of blessing, we thank you for our public libraries. We ask that you increase in our land knowledge and wisdom. We thank you for institutions that meet the needs of all people.
Silence
Blessed are you, O Lord;
You supply all our needs.

God of blessing, you are the hope of the hopeless; you give sleep to the anxious and wholeness to those who feel alone. Comfort and care for those in need of your healing touch this day.
Invite the congregation to add their petitions, followed by silence
Blessed are you, O Lord;
You supply all our needs.

God of blessing, you make us heirs of eternal life through your blessed Son. May we be made like him in his eternal and glorious Kingdom. We trust to you our dead, praying especially today for all those who died for the causes of freedom and peace.
Silence
Blessed are you, O Lord;
You supply all our needs.

Following the example of Hannah, let us pour out our souls as an offering to the Lord, praying, "My heart exults in you, O God; *for you hear the prayer of your faithful ones.*"

Holy One, you have placed your law in our hearts; you remember our sins no more; you have washed us clean with the pure waters of baptism: may we provoke one another to love and good deeds.
Invite the congregation to add their thanksgivings, followed by silence
My heart exults in you, O God;
For you hear the prayer of your faithful ones.

Holy One, you raise the poor from the dust; you make the hungry fat with spoil: give us faith to trust in your faithfulness; give us faith to trust you with our possessions, our loved ones, and our lives.
Silence
My heart exults in you, O God;
For you hear the prayer of your faithful ones.

Holy One, centuries of war and famine have exhausted the planet and the people. Change our hearts; renew our planet; give us peace.
Silence
My heart exults in you, O God;
For you hear the prayer of your faithful ones.

Holy One, you break the bows of the mighty and you strengthen the feeble. You weigh the actions of the arrogant and you strengthen those in positions of authority: guide all who govern and hold authority in our land, especially our local leaders.
Silence
My heart exults in you, O God;
For you hear the prayer of your faithful ones.

Holy One, you lift up the needy: hear the prayers of the troubled and the anxious— comfort especially those who long to bear children but cannot.
Invite the congregation to add their petitions, followed by silence
My heart exults in you, O God;
For you hear the prayer of your faithful ones.

Holy One, you are the God of life: may we embrace and ever hold fast the blessed hope of everlasting life, which you have given us in our Savior Jesus Christ.
Silence
My heart exults in you, O God;
For you hear the prayer of your faithful ones.

Grace to you and peace from him who is and who was and who is to come. Let us rejoice in the King of kings, praying, "You have made us to be a kingdom, *to you be glory and dominion forever and ever.*"

Everlasting King, you have freed us from our sins and made us a people: clothe your priests with righteousness; let your faithful people sing with joy.
Invite the congregation to add their thanksgivings, followed by silence
You have made us to be a kingdom,
To you be glory and dominion forever and ever.

Everlasting King, you came into the world to testify to the truth. May the words of truth overcome the euphemisms and hyperbole that dominate and control your people.
Silence
You have made us to be a kingdom,
To you be glory and dominion forever and ever.

Everlasting King, mercifully grant that the peoples of the earth, divided and enslaved by sin, may be freed and brought together under your most gracious rule.
Silence
You have made us to be a kingdom,
To you be glory and dominion forever and ever.

Everlasting King, your reign is one of justice and truth: bless those who strive for justice. Bless those who yearn for truth.
Silence
You have made us to be a kingdom,
To you be glory and dominion forever and ever.

Everlasting King, you love us. It is your will to restore all things. Restore to health and wholeness all those who suffer.
Invite the congregation to add their petitions, followed by silence
You have made us to be a kingdom,
To you be glory and dominion forever and ever.

Everlasting King, you are the faithful witness, the firstborn of the dead: raise us, with all your saints, to rule with you forever and ever. Amen.
Silence
You have made us to be a kingdom,
To you be glory and dominion forever and ever.

YEAR C

My brothers and sisters, may God strengthen your hearts in holiness. Trusting in God, let us pray, "O come, o come, Emmanuel; *be our hope and our salvation.*"

God our hope, make us increase and abound in love for one another. Keep your Church on the paths of love and faithfulness.
Silence
O come, o come, Emmanuel;
Be our hope and our salvation.

God our hope, usher in your reign of justice and righteousness. May all the world know your peace and safety.
Silence
O come, o come, Emmanuel;
Be our hope and our salvation.

God our hope, you place signs in the sun, the moon, and the stars. Give us the eyes to see, the wisdom to prepare, and the faith to trust in you.
Silence
O come, o come, Emmanuel;
Be our hope and our salvation.

God our hope, under your reign divisions are overcome, unity restored: bring the people of this region—from city, village and town—together in a spirit of love and respect.
Invite the congregation to add their thanksgivings, followed by silence
O come, o come, Emmanuel;
Be our hope and our salvation.

God our hope, remember your compassion and love. Heal and restore the sick and the suffering, the anxious and the grieving.
Invite the congregation to add their petitions, followed by silence
O come, o come, Emmanuel;
Be our hope and our salvation.

God our hope, keep us blameless before you that we may meet the coming of our Lord Jesus with joy. May we, and all who have died, rise to life immortal with all your saints.
Silence
O come, o come, Emmanuel;
Be our hope and our salvation.

I am confident of this, that the one who began a good work among you will bring it to completion by the day of Jesus Christ. Prepare your hearts for his arrival, praying, "Fill the valleys, make low the hills; *come, great Redeemer, come.*"

Merciful God, increase our love to overflowing. Make your Church pure and blameless that we may greet with joy the coming of our Lord Jesus Christ.
Silence
Fill the valleys, make low the hills;
Come, great Redeemer, come.

Merciful God, we long for the light of hope to break into our world, to shine on those who dwell in darkness and the shadow of death, to guide us into the way of peace.
Silence
Fill the valleys, make low the hills;
Come, great Redeemer, come.

Merciful God, give us grace to heed the warnings of those calling us to be better stewards of your creation. We thank you for all you have made, especially those things that sustain and better our lives.
Silence
Fill the valleys, make low the hills;
Come, great Redeemer, come.

Merciful God, you lead us with joy; you delight in our joy. You clothe us in beauty. We give you thanks for your tender care.
Invite the congregation to add their thanksgivings, followed by silence
Fill the valleys, make low the hills;
Come, great Redeemer, come.

Merciful God, you remember your children. You do not leave us in sorrow or affliction. Crown your children with glory; clothe them with righteousness.
Invite the congregation to add their petitions, followed by silence
Fill the valleys, make low the hills;
Come, great Redeemer, come.

Merciful God, you have raised up for us salvation through your Son. Keep us, with all your saints, in the eternal life of Christ.
Silence
Fill the valleys, make low the hills;
Come, great Redeemer, come.

Rejoice in the Lord always; again I will say, rejoice. Surely, it is God who saves us; therefore, we joyfully pray to the Lord, "God our salvation: *thank you.*"

Though hindered by our sins and in need of your bountiful grace and mercy, you never leave us. You are ever in our midst. Renew your Church in love.
Invite the congregation to add their thanksgivings, followed by silence
God our salvation:
Thank you.

Make your deeds known among the people, O God. Save the lame; gather the outcast. May the exiles know home and all people know your peace.
Silence
God our salvation:
Thank you.

May your springs of salvation renew the earth. Heal our planet and restore in us a sense of responsibility and gratitude.
Silence
God our salvation:
Thank you.

Merciful God, in this month of great excess and consumerism, call the financial and business communities to act justly and generously. Grant that those without coats be clothed and those without food be fed.
Silence
God our salvation:
Thank you.

O God, you have done great things. With thankful hearts we pray to you for those burdened by shame, grief, or weakness. Be for them a stronghold and a sure defense.
Invite the congregation to add their petitions, followed by silence
God our salvation:
Thank you.

God our salvation, gather us, with all those who have died, into your sacred heart. Grant us to sing your praises for all eternity.
Silence
God our salvation:
Thank you.

The Mighty One has done great things for us. And so we appeal to God once again, praying, "Stir up your strength, O Lord; *and come to help us.*"

Prepare in us a mansion for yourself, O Christ.
Silence
Stir up your strength, O Lord;
And come to help us.

Restore us, O God of hosts. May we know security. May we know peace. May we know the benefits of the reign of your Christ.
Silence
Stir up your strength, O Lord;
And come to help us.

Show the strength of your arm, O God: lift up the lowly. Fill the hungry with good things. Look on your children with favor.
Silence
Stir up your strength, O Lord;
And come to help us.

Have mercy on all captives and prisoners, O God. Remember them and come to their aid. Fill our hearts with mercy. May we learn to forgive even as you forgive us.
Invite the congregation to add their thanksgivings, followed by silence
Stir up your strength, O Lord;
And come to help us.

Hear the prayers of your people, O God of hosts. May those who have fed on the bread of tears, feed instead on your strength, O Lord. Show them the light of your countenance and be their salvation.
Invite the congregation to add their petitions, followed by silence
Stir up your strength, O Lord;
And come to help us.

Great Shepherd, gather your flock into your eternal kingdom. Bless the dying, embrace the dead, and comfort those who mourn.
Silence
Stir up your strength, O Lord;
And come to help us.

Come let us adore Christ, the Lord. Let us pray, "Glorious Lord, *grant us your peace.*"

Christ the Lord, we humbly adore you: make joyful our hearts. Strengthen your Church with humility and faith that we might triumph over the power of evil.
Silence
Glorious Lord,
Grant us your peace.

Christ the Lord, we humbly adore you: you abhor neither the simple nor the lowly. Shine your light on all the world that the nations may look upon your truth and find their salvation.
Silence
Glorious Lord,
Grant us your peace.

Christ the Lord, we humbly adore you: may all of creation burst forth in songs of praise. May all the works of your hand glorify you.
Invite the congregation to add their thanksgivings, followed by silence
Glorious Lord,
Grant us your peace.

Christ the Lord, we humbly adore you: summon the people of the city to yourself. May all of the distractions and heartache of our lives fade away in the joy of your presence.
Silence
Glorious Lord,
Grant us your peace.

Christ the Lord, we humbly adore you: you love us so dearly. Grant your healing grace to sinners, to the poor, to those in need of love. Open your arms to the sick and the lonely.
Invite the congregation to add their petitions, followed by silence
Glorious Lord,
Grant us your peace.

Christ the Lord, we humbly adore you: all glory be given to you. You blessed our earthly bodies with your birth; and you promise to raise us to new life by your death and resurrection.
Silence
Glorious Lord,
Grant us your peace.

Christmas 1

The Word became flesh and lived among us, and we have seen his glory, the glory as of a father's only son, full of grace and truth. We are witnesses, praying, "Shine forth in our lives, O Lord. *Hallelujah!*"

Abba, Father, you have received us as your children. Make our hearts shine ever brighter with the pure light of Christ, that all people might witness your all-encompassing love.
Silence
Shine forth in our lives, O Lord.
Hallelujah!

Almighty God, let all the nations witness your glory. Cause righteousness and praise to cover the earth.
Silence
Shine forth in our lives, O Lord.
Hallelujah!

Great Lord, you are mighty in power: you graciously make the earth to burst forth with green plants; you provide food for flocks and herds; you give us the resources to thrive on this planet. May we be thankful in our hearts and generous in our lives.
Invite the congregation to add their thanksgivings, followed by silence
Shine forth in our lives, O Lord.
Hallelujah!

O God, it is you who establishes peace. Comfort your people with safety and security; assure us that it is not by our own strength, but by your goodness, that we can rest in quiet confidence.
Silence
Shine forth in our lives, O Lord.
Hallelujah!

Loving God, you are the healer of the brokenhearted; it is you who binds up their wounds; you lift up the lowly. Clothe your children with the garments of health and salvation.
Invite the congregation to add their petitions, followed by silence
Shine forth in our lives, O Lord.
Hallelujah!

O God, you sent your Son to redeem us from sin and death: draw us closer to your Son Jesus—into your heart, both now and in the life to come.
Silence
Shine forth in our lives, O Lord.
Hallelujah!

Sisters and brothers, let the same mind be in you that was in Christ Jesus. With humble hearts let us say to the Lord, "Lord Jesus, *we bow our hearts at your name.*"

Jesus, we exalt your name in all the world! Bless your Church. Inspire us by the Holy Spirit to confess you as Lord over all we are, all we do and all we hope to do.
Silence
Lord Jesus,
We bow our hearts at your name.

Jesus, we exalt your name in all the world! Bless the people of the world. May the whole world experience your peace.
Silence
Lord Jesus,
We bow our hearts at your name.

Jesus, we exalt your name in all the world! Bless our planet. Make us faithful stewards of all the works of your fingers. Forgive us when we fail to respect your creatures: the beasts of the field, the birds of the air, and the fish of the sea.
Silence
Lord Jesus,
We bow our hearts at your name.

Jesus, we exalt your name in all the world! Bless our city and our region. Give us renewed hope and purpose as we begin this new year.
Silence
Lord Jesus,
We bow our hearts at your name.

Jesus, we exalt your name in all the world! Bless the sick and the lonely and all those in great need. Make your face to shine on them and be gracious to them.
Invite the congregation to add their petitions and thanksgivings, followed by silence
Lord Jesus,
We bow our hearts at your name.

Jesus, we exalt your name in all the world! Bless the dying and the dead. We praise you that through your death on the cross you have earned for us everlasting life.
Silence
Lord Jesus,
We bow our hearts at your name.

Christmas 2

The Lord God is both sun and shield; God will give grace and glory. In the house of our God, let us pray, "Lord God of hosts, *hear our prayer.*"

We give thanks for your Church, O God. Bless it with every spiritual blessing in the heavenly places. May we be made happy in the knowledge of the hope to which we are called.
Invite the congregation to add their thanksgivings, followed by silence
Lord God of hosts,
Hear our prayer.

We give thanks for this nation, O God. Give to our leaders a spirit of wisdom. Deliver them from selfish ambition and give all the people a heart for your children, especially those little ones living in poverty or exile.
Silence
Lord God of hosts;
Hear our prayer.

We give thanks for your creation, O God. Where there is desolation, bring forth springs of clean water. Where your creatures are without a place, may they find their refuge in you.
Silence
Lord God of hosts,
Hear our prayer.

We give thanks for this city, O God. Set us on a straight path where we shall not stumble. Bring new life to languishing areas.
Silence
Lord God of hosts,
Hear our prayer.

We give thanks for all those in our lives, O God. We pray especially for those who know weeping and tears. Turn their mourning into joy, comfort them, and give them gladness for sorrow.
Invite the congregation to add their petitions, followed by silence
Lord God of hosts,
Hear our prayer.

We give thanks for the saints at rest, O God. Gather them into your great heavenly company. May they enjoy forever the riches of your glorious inheritance.
Silence
Lord God of hosts,
Hear our prayer.

Arise, shine; for your light has come, and the glory of the Lord has risen upon you. We pray as pilgrims, "Lead us to your presence; *let us see your glory!*"

Almighty God, grant to your Church wisdom. Work through us that we might lead many to the knowledge and love of you.
Silence
Lead us to your presence;
Let us see your glory.

Defend the needy, Lord Christ. Rescue the poor and thwart all the ways of oppression.
Silence
Lead us to your presence;
Let us see your glory.

The heavens reveal your wonders, O God. Give us eyes to see, hearts to follow, and lives that pay you homage.
Invite the congregation to add their thanksgivings, followed by silence
Lead us to your presence;
Let us see your glory.

Bless all students as they return to school and university. May they find wisdom as well as knowledge; give them a hunger for your truth.
Silence
Lead us to your presence;
Let us see your glory.

Loving God, you are the help of the helpless and the deliverer of those in distress: bless and heal all those in need.
Invite the congregation to add their petitions, followed by silence
Lead us to your presence;
Let us see your glory.

Great redeemer, you have guided us to your presence; you have shown us your glory. Grant us, that we might at last, see you face to face.
Silence
Lead us to your presence;
Let us see your glory.

Epiphany 1C: The Baptism of Our Lord

The Lord shall give us the blessings of strength and peace. Beloved of God, let us pray, "Walk with us through the waters, O God; *walk with us through the fire.*"

Deliver your Church, O God, from fear. Strengthen those you have redeemed by your presence. Give us all the courage to keep our baptismal promises.
Silence
Walk with us through the waters, O God;
Walk with us through the fire.

O God, you have blessed us to be members of your household. Strengthen the unity of the Church—those serving you in the east, west, north, and south.
Silence
Walk with us through the waters, O God;
Walk with us through the fire.

Your power, O God, is evident in the mysteries of our universe. By water and your Holy Spirit you have made us a new people. We give you thanks and praise.
Invite the congregation to add their thanksgivings, followed by silence
Walk with us through the waters, O God;
Walk with us through the fire.

Break down the walls of division in our city and our nation. Bring us together as one human family, formed and made by your great hands.
Silence
Walk with us through the waters, O God;
Walk with us through the fire.

Heal and comfort your beloved children, O God. Be with the needy in their trials. May they know that they are precious in your sight.
Invite the congregation to add their petitions, followed by silence
Walk with us through the waters, O God;
Walk with us through the fire.

Heavenly Parent, you have accepted us as your children. You have made us heirs with Christ. In your great mercy, receive us, and all who have died, into glory everlasting.
Silence
Walk with us through the waters, O God;
Walk with us through the fire.

The glory of the Lord has been revealed that we might see and believe. Trusting in the Lord, let us pray, "Jesus Christ, Light of the world, *in your light we see light.*"

Blessed Lord, through the Spirit you have given to your Church varieties of gifts. Bind us together as your body and then use us, we pray, to show forth your great light.
Silence
Jesus Christ, Light of the world,
In your light we see light.

Blessed Lord, your righteousness is like the strong mountains and your justice is like the great deep. May all the peoples of the earth look to you for salvation.
Silence
Jesus Christ, Light of the world,
In your light we see light.

Blessed Lord, restore desolate lands. Renew your creation to bring forth life and growth.
Invite the congregation to add their thanksgivings, followed by silence
Jesus Christ, Light of the world,
In your light we see light.

May we desire the common good. We pray, blessed Lord, that you will teach us to love each other. We thank you for the diversity with which you have gifted the human family and bless you for the hope of unity.
Invite the congregation to add their thanksgivings, followed by silence
Jesus Christ, Light of the world,
In your light we see light.

Continue your loving-kindness to those who know you, blessed Lord. Heal and restore those who are sick or weak in body, mind, or spirit.
Invite the congregation to add their petitions, followed by silence
Jesus Christ, Light of the world,
In your light we see light.

Blessed Lord, with you is the well of life. By water and the Spirit you accept us as members of your family. By the springs of your living water preserve us for life eternal.
Silence
Jesus Christ, Light of the world,
In your light we see light.

Now you are the body of Christ and individually members of it. Empowered by the Spirit, let us pray together saying, "We bless you, Lord our God. *Amen, amen.*"

Let the words of our mouths and the meditations of our hearts be acceptable in your sight, O Lord, our strength and our redeemer.
Silence
We bless you, Lord our God.
Amen, amen.

By the spirit of the Lord, may we, your Church, carry on the work of Jesus. Open our hearts to the poor and the captives, to the blind and the oppressed.
Silence
We bless you, Lord our God.
Amen, amen.

The heavens declare your glory, Great Creator, and the firmament shows your handiwork. We praise you and we thank you for the beauty and majesty of your creation.
Invite the congregation to add their thanksgivings, followed by silence
We bless you, Lord our God.
Amen, amen.

We thank you, O God, for the many members that make up our body; for the gifts, the work, and the prayers we share. We ask you to bless especially our leaders, lay and ordained. Give us wisdom and guide by your Spirit.
Silence
We bless you, Lord our God.
Amen, amen.

We pray for those who are sick or sorrowful. When they suffer, we suffer with them. Revive and heal them, we pray. May your joy be their strength.
Invite the congregation to add their petitions, followed by silence
We bless you, Lord our God.
Amen, amen.

O God, you have formed an eternal bond with us in baptism. Whether living or dead, bless and keep your children forever.
Silence
We bless you, Lord our God.
Amen, amen.

Happy are the ones who put their trust in God! Presenting our prayers and our hearts to God, let us pray, "Lord God of Hosts, hear our prayer; *hearken, O God of Jacob.*"

Fill the members of your Church, O God, with a longing and desire for your presence. Fill us with joy as we approach your altar. Sustain us as we go forth in the name of your Christ.
Invite the congregation to add their thanksgivings, followed by silence
Lord God of Hosts, hear our prayer;
Hearken, O God of Jacob.

Bless those, O God, who walk with integrity. Give them the strength to stand for truth in an age of deception and spin.
Silence
Lord God of Hosts, hear our prayer;
Hearken, O God of Jacob.

Almighty God, spring forth new life in desolate places. Restore the beauty and health of your creation.
Silence
Lord God of Hosts, hear our prayer;
Hearken, O God of Jacob.

O Lord, you are both sun and shield. On this city shed your light that we might see our best future. Protect us from the forces of violence and hatred that threaten to undermine the future you want for us.
Silence
Lord God of Hosts, hear our prayer;
Hearken, O God of Jacob.

Merciful and faithful God, we present to you our brothers and sisters who are now in pain and sorrow. We trust them to your mercy, asking that you would heal them.
Invite the congregation to add their petitions, followed by silence
Lord God of Hosts, hear our prayer;
Hearken, O God of Jacob.

Loving God, you sent your Son Jesus to share our human nature, to share our flesh and blood, to share even our suffering and death. We pray for those who suffer and die in the service of others. Grant them your everlasting peace.
Silence
Lord God of Hosts, hear our prayer;
Hearken, O God of Jacob.

Epiphany 4C

My fellow pilgrims, the Lord is our strong rock, a castle to keep us safe. In confidence, let us pray, "In you, O Lord, have we taken refuge; *let us never be ashamed.*"

Increase our love, O God. Deliver your Church from boastfulness and arrogance. Fill us instead with patience and kindness.
Silence
In you, O Lord, have we taken refuge;
Let us never be ashamed.

Increase our love, O God. Deliver this nation from pride and fear. Give us eyes to see your hand at work in all nations and peoples. God, bless the world.
Silence
In you, O Lord, have we taken refuge;
Let us never be ashamed.

Increase our love, O God. Let it not be limited only to other human beings but spread to all that you have made.
Invite the congregation to add their thanksgivings, followed by silence
In you, O Lord, have we taken refuge;
Let us never be ashamed.

Increase our love, O God. May we seek and serve Christ in our neighbors, in family, friends, and strangers.
Silence
In you, O Lord, have we taken refuge;
Let us never be ashamed.

Increase our love, O God. By the power of your great love, heal those who are ill; strengthen those who are struggling to endure great pain. We pray that, as we lift our brothers and sisters to you in prayer, they will, even now, feel our love.
Invite the congregation to add their petitions, followed by silence
In you, O Lord, have we taken refuge;
Let us never be ashamed.

Increase our trust in your love, O God. May those who have died find in your presence everlasting and overwhelming love.
Silence
In you, O Lord, have we taken refuge;
Let us never be ashamed.

Sisters and brothers, wholeheartedly give thanks to the Lord. Trusting in our Great Creator, let us pray, "Ever-living God, inspire us with new life; *inspire us with your light.*"

Bless the people of this [diocese], O Lover of Souls. Call us to greater devotion and service. Fan the flame of the Holy Spirit within us, that we might be set ablaze with the fire of your love.
Silence
Ever-living God, inspire us with new life;
Inspire us with your light.

Make known your ways of justice and truth, Almighty God. Bring the powers of this world to their knees and establish your kingdom of peace on the earth.
Silence
Ever-living God, inspire us with new life;
Inspire us with your light.

Loving Creator, do not abandon the works of your hands. Sustain this planet and all its creatures. Give us creative minds and generous hearts as we live and move within your creation.
Silence
Ever-living God, inspire us with new life;
Inspire us with your light.

We thank you for the communities in which we live and work and worship. Make us witnesses of your love and faithfulness.
Invite the congregation to add their thanksgivings, followed by silence
Ever-living God, inspire us with new life;
Inspire us with your light.

O Lord, you care for the lowly. You hear our cries for mercy; you increase the strength of the weak. We offer our prayers for those in need of your healing and your grace.
Invite the congregation to add their petitions, followed by silence
Ever-living God, inspire us with new life;
Inspire us with your light.

Gracious God, your love endures forever and so we pray for those who have died, trusting them to your everlasting care.
Silence
Ever-living God, inspire us with new life;
Inspire us with your light.

Blessed are those who trust in the Lord! So lift up the prayers of your heart, saying, "Test our minds; search our hearts; *hear our prayer.*"

Lord our God, bless your Church. Bless us with the boldness of the prophets. Give us the courage to proclaim your kingdom. Give us the courage to proclaim our allegiance to Christ alone.
Silence
Test our minds; search our hearts;
Hear our prayer.

Lord our God, bless the people of this and every nation. Bless us with compassion for the poor, the hungry, and those who weep. Turn our hearts away from our selfish desires; turn our hearts to you.
Silence
Test our minds; search our hearts;
Hear our prayer.

Lord our God, bless this planet, your very footstool. Bless this planet with growth and health. Give food enough that the hungry might be filled.
Silence
Test our minds; search our hearts;
Hear our prayer.

Lord our God, bless our city. Bless us with health. Heal our land and our water. Deliver us from violence and sorrow.
Silence
Test our minds; search our hearts;
Hear our prayer.

Lord our God, bless the sick and the struggling. Send forth your healing power. Cause laughter to once again flow from the hearts of those who now weep.
Invite the congregation to add their petitions and thanksgivings, followed by silence
Test our minds; search our hearts;
Hear our prayer.

Lord our God, bless the dying and the dead. Bless them with everlasting life. And at the last day raise them to new life with your Christ.
Silence
Test our minds; search our hearts;
Hear our prayer.

Sisters and brothers, do to others as you would have them do to you. Let us pray for others, saying, "We have come before you, O God; *and here will we wait for you.*"

Merciful God, help us to love our enemies, to do good to those who hate us. It is a hard thing for us. Make us merciful, just as you are merciful.
Silence
We have come before you, O God;
And here will we wait for you.

Holy God, make your justice shine like the noonday sun. Vindicate the meek; save the righteous; rescue those who find their refuge in you.
Silence
We have come before you, O God;
And here will we wait for you.

We pray, Creator God, for those who experience the pangs of hunger. We cry to you for those dying of starvation. Bless them with provision. Give us a new appreciation for the abundance in our lives.
Invite the congregation to add their thanksgivings, followed by silence
We have come before you, O God;
And here will we wait for you.

Heal families. Heal our families. Heal the families in our community. Mend our divisions. Make us ministers of reconciliation.
Silence
We have come before you, O God;
And here will we wait for you.

Heal these bodies, O God, that you have made from the dust of the earth. Deliver us, and those for whom we now pray, from our infirmities.
Invite the congregation to add their petitions, followed by silence
We have come before you, O God;
And here will we wait for you.

Raise in power those who have died in weakness, mighty Redeemer. Raise to imperishability those who have died in the flesh. Raise those whose bodies have returned to the dust to greater and eternal glory.
Silence
We have come before you, O God;
And here will we wait for you.

Beloved, be steadfast, always excelling in the work of the Lord, because in the Lord your labor is not in vain. Neither are your prayers, so let us pray. "Thank you, Lord. *In your presence, we shout for joy!*"

Establish your Church, O God, on a well-built foundation, the foundation of your Son Jesus Christ. Bless us with good and faithful leaders. Accomplish through us your perfect purpose.
Silence
Thank you, Lord.
In your presence, we shout for joy!

Establish your kingdom here on earth, O God. We long for the day when the people of the earth will finally live in joy and peace.
Silence
Thank you, Lord.
In your presence, we shout for joy!

Make the earth spring forth with fruitful plants, generous God. Water the earth; give seeds to the sower and bread to the eater.
Invite the congregation to add their thanksgivings, followed by silence
Thank you, Lord.
In your presence, we shout for joy!

Forgive us, O Lord, when we prove hypocritical. Give us the wisdom to see our own flaws, so that we might not injure or harm our neighbors.
Silence
Thank you, Lord.
In your presence, we shout for joy!

You, O Lord, make us glad by the work of your hands; at the work of your hands we sing for joy. Touch those who now suffer; heal and deliver them.
Invite the congregation to add their petitions, followed by silence
Thank you, Lord.
In your presence, we shout for joy!

You, O God, have, through the death and resurrection of your Son, taken away the sting of death. Death has been swallowed up in victory. We rejoice in you, O God, and we await that glorious day when the dead shall be raised imperishable.
Silence
Thank you, Lord.
In your presence, we shout for joy!

Proclaim the greatness of the Lord our God, for the Lord our God is the Holy One. Placing our hope in God, offering ourselves to God, let us pray, "Shine in our hearts, Lord Jesus, *and transform our lives.*"

Almighty God, as we turn our gaze toward our Lenten journey, strengthen us to bear our cross and to follow faithfully in the way of your Son, Jesus.
Silence
Shine in our hearts, Lord Jesus,
And transform our lives.

O mighty King, lover of justice, establish equity, that the dignity of every human being may be preserved and respected. But also show us mercy and forgive us for our failures.
Silence
Shine in our hearts, Lord Jesus,
And transform our lives.

Your glory outshines the brightness of the sun; the earth shakes in your presence and yet, it pleases you, O God, to reveal yourself to us through your creation. Give us hearts that love what you call good.
Invite the congregation to add their thanksgivings, followed by silence
Shine in our hearts, Lord Jesus,
And transform our lives.

We pray for all those in need of your liberating salvation, O God. May the glory we encounter here shine on our faces and in our lives. Strengthen us to embody the Good News of your love.
Silence
Shine in our hearts, Lord Jesus,
And transform our lives.

Lord Jesus, free the suffering from their afflictions. Restore the broken to wholeness. Unveil the faces of those who dwell in great darkness.
Invite the congregation to add their petitions, followed by silence
Shine in our hearts, Lord Jesus,
And transform our lives.

May we be changed into the likeness of your Son, O God, from glory to glory. Bring us at last into that place, with all your saints, where we might no longer see in a mirror dimly, but see you face to face.
Silence
Shine in our hearts, Lord Jesus,
And transform our lives.

Everyone who calls on the name of the Lord shall be saved. Our generous God hears us when we pray; therefore, let us pray, "Hear us, O God; *save us, O God.*"

You know your Church, O God. You know that because of fear and greed, we are slow to offer the first fruits of our hearts. Forgive us and come quickly to help us.
Silence
Hear us, O God;
Save us, O God.

You know the hearts of mortals, O God. You know that we are prone to hatred and division. Yet, you make no distinctions, but only love. Help us to be more like you. Forgive us and come quickly to help us.
Silence
Hear us, O God;
Save us, O God.

You know we are quick to exploit your creation, O God. You know we take the blessings of this life for granted. Forgive us and come quickly to help us.
Invite the congregation to add their thanksgivings, followed by silence
Hear us, O God;
Save us, O God.

You know our temptations, O God. You know we are not as strong as we think we are. Give us your strength. Forgive us and come quickly to help us.
Silence
Hear us, O God;
Save us, O God.

You know our weaknesses, O God. You know we struggle in our pain; we suffer and experience trouble. Come quickly to help us.
Invite the congregation to add their petitions, followed by silence
Hear us, O God;
Save us, O God.

In you, O God, do we put our trust. We entrust to you our dead because you alone are our refuge and salvation. You alone are mighty to save.
Silence
Hear us, O God;
Save us, O God.

Brothers and sisters, wait patiently for the Lord. Trusting our merciful God to hear us, we pray, "Hearken to our voice, O Lord, when we call; *have mercy on us and answer us.*"

Almighty God, we thank you that by water and the Holy Spirit you have made us citizens of your heavenly kingdom. Show us your ways, O Lord, and give us the strength to stand firm.
Silence
Hearken to our voice, O Lord, when we call;
Have mercy on us and answer us.

Forgive us, gracious God, for the violence and anger in our own hearts. Open our ears and hearts to listen to your prophets and heed their call to repentance.
Silence
Hearken to our voice, O Lord, when we call;
Have mercy on us and answer us.

We long, O God, to behold your fair beauty. Open our eyes to the beauty all around us. Inspire our hearts to sing out and make music to you.
Invite the congregation to add their thanksgivings, followed by silence
Hearken to our voice, O Lord, when we call;
Have mercy on us and answer us.

We pray, O God, for all those who have no place to call home. In their day of trouble keep them safe in your shelter; hide them in your dwelling. May they find housing in this life and find their home in your heart forever.
Silence
Hearken to our voice, O Lord, when we call;
Have mercy on us and answer us.

Lord Jesus, you desire to gather your children as a hen gathers her brood under her wings. Be the light and salvation of those who are lost and alone. May all in need know your goodness and mercy.
Invite the congregation to add their petitions, followed by silence
Hearken to our voice, O Lord, when we call;
Have mercy on us and answer us.

Lord Jesus, in the fullness of time make all things subject to yourself and transform us, with all your saints , that at the last we might be conformed to your glorious likeness.
Silence
Hearken to our voice, O Lord, when we call;
Have mercy on us and answer us.

Brothers and sisters, our God is faithful. Let us offer our prayers to God, saying, "God, your loving-kindness is better than life itself; *we bless you and we praise you.*"

O God, you are our God; eagerly we seek you; our souls thirst for you, our flesh faints for you, as in a parched and barren land. Refresh your Church, revive your Church with living water.
Invite the congregation to add their thanksgivings, followed by silence
God, your loving-kindness is better than life itself;
We bless you and we praise you.

Faithful God, be the comfort and strength of innocent victims and their families. We pray for all those who die suddenly and unprepared.
Silence
God, your loving-kindness is better than life itself;
We bless you and we praise you.

Great Mountain God, open our eyes to your presence in the world around us. Set the fire of your presence before us and lead our feet to holy ground.
Silence
God, your loving-kindness is better than life itself;
We bless you and we praise you.

We pray, O God, for victims of sexual violence and abuse. Deliver them; heal their wounds and scars; restore innocence and the ability to trust. Purify our own hearts that we may honor and respect each other.
Silence
God, your loving-kindness is better than life itself;
We bless you and we praise you.

O God, you are our helper; you hide us under the mighty shadow of your wings. Defend your children from all adversities which may happen to the body or soul.
Invite the congregation to add their petitions, followed by silence
God, your loving-kindness is better than life itself;
We bless you and we praise you.

God of Abraham, Isaac and Jacob, God of our fathers and mothers, feed us with spiritual food; refresh us with spiritual drink. Preserve us, with all your saints, forever.
Silence
God, your loving-kindness is better than life itself;
We bless you and we praise you.

Be glad and rejoice in the Lord; shout for joy, all you who are true of heart. Having been reconciled to God through Christ Jesus, let us pray, "Lord, let your mercy embrace us; *accept our prayer."*

Gracious God, you have entrusted to your Church the ministry of reconciliation. Reconcile our members to you and to each other, and then work through us to embrace the world.
Silence
Lord, let your mercy embrace us;
Accept our prayer.

Open our hearts to welcome sinners as you welcome us. Give us eyes to see others, not from a human point of view, but as you see them.
Silence
Lord, let your mercy embrace us;
Accept our prayer.

Jesus, you are the true bread which gives life to the world: evermore give us this bread that our souls may be satisfied. And satisfy our bodies with abundant produce from the land.
Invite the congregation to add their thanksgivings, followed by silence
Lord, let your mercy embrace us;
Accept our prayer.

We pray, O God, for families. Restore broken relationships. Heal those who have suffered betrayal and alienation. Comfort those for whom reconciliation in this life is not possible. Shield those with reason to celebrate.
Silence
Lord, let your mercy embrace us;
Accept our prayer.

You, O God, are a hiding place for those in trouble: you deliver the oppressed; you forgive the guilty; you roll away the disgrace of your people. We make our prayers to you for those in trouble.
Invite the congregation to add their petitions, followed by silence
Lord, let your mercy embrace us;
Accept our prayer.

Holy Jesus, it is our prayer that you may live in us, and we in you, both in this mortal life and for all eternity.
Silence
Lord, let your mercy embrace us;
Accept our prayer.

Lent 5C

Sisters and brothers, the Lord has done great things for us. With glad and thankful hearts, let us pray, "Fix our hearts where joy is found; *Lord, hear our prayer.*"

Do a new thing in your Church, O Lord. From our dry places spring forth new life. Refresh your bishops, priests, and deacons. Refresh all Christians in their vocations.
Invite the congregation to add their thanksgivings, followed by silence
Fix our hearts where joy is found;
Lord, hear our prayer.

Restore the dreams of those who have lost hope. Among the swift and varied changes of the world, be a strong foundation on which all can rely.
Silence
Fix our hearts where joy is found;
Lord, hear our prayer.

Give water in dry places. Remove the suffering of those who live with drought. Bring water, quench thirst, and give growth in desperate lands.
Silence
Fix our hearts where joy is found;
Lord, hear our prayer.

We pray, O God, for the poor. Be merciful to victims of theft. Restore the fortunes of those devastated by dishonest men and women. Never forget the lives of your poor.
Silence
Fix our hearts where joy is found;
Lord, hear our prayer.

Let those who sow with tears, reap with songs of joy. Fill down-turned mouths with shouts of joyful deliverance. Restore your people, O Lord.
Invite the congregation to add their petitions, followed by silence
Fix our hearts where joy is found;
Lord, hear our prayer.

O God, we long to know Christ and the power of his resurrection. Even as we share in his suffering, even as we die, may we, and all who die, attain the resurrection of the dead.
Silence
Fix our hearts where joy is found;
Lord, hear our prayer.

Brothers and sisters, are we not wholly reliant on God's tender love and mercy? So let us cry out to our Lord, saying, "Look upon us in mercy; *and with compassion remember us.*"

Have mercy on your Church, O Lord, for the times we have denied you. We have not been humble as you are humble. We are too often quick to speak and slow to love.
Silence
Look upon us in mercy;
And with compassion remember us.

Have mercy on those who hold authority in the nations of the world, O Lord, especially those who are threatened by your message of love and mercy. Forgive us for our silence and complicity.
Silence
Look upon us in mercy;
And with compassion remember us.

Have mercy on those of us who are called to be stewards of your creation, O Lord. We have exploited and mistreated your masterpiece. Teach us to love what you have called good.
Silence
Look upon us in mercy;
And with compassion remember us.

Have mercy on our enemies, O Lord, and on those who persecute us. Teach us the love of Jesus, who from the cross prayed, "Father, forgive them."
Silence
Look upon us in mercy;
And with compassion remember us.

Have mercy on all who are sick and suffering, O Lord. Strengthen the afflicted. Comfort and care for those wasted with grief. Make your face to shine upon your servants.
Invite the congregation to add their petitions and thanksgivings, followed by silence
Look upon us in mercy;
And with compassion remember us.

Merciful Lord, you became obedient to death, even death upon a cross. Even as you have shared our mortality, mercifully grant us to share in your resurrection.
Silence
Look upon us in mercy;
And with compassion remember us.

Jesus Christ is risen today, our triumphant holy day. Alleluia! So let us pray to our Lord, saying, "To you we offer praise eternal; *Alleluia! Alleluia!*"

Heavenly King, for us you endured the cross and the grave. When we were yet sinners, you redeemed and saved us. May we sing your eternal praises everywhere we go.
Silence
To you we offer praise eternal;
Alleluia! Alleluia!

Incarnate Love, where hearts are wintry, grieving, or in pain, call forth new life by your touch. Bring forth life in the barren places of this world.
Silence
To you we offer praise eternal;
Alleluia! Alleluia!

Author of Life, you are the ruler of creation. All things created on earth sing to your glory. From the death of the winter, raise the fair beauty of earth.
Silence
To you we offer praise eternal;
Alleluia! Alleluia!

Living Savior, you hold the future. You bless and restore our families, our communities, our world with babies and children. Though they face uncertain days, we trust them to the certainty of your endless and eternal love.
Silence
To you we offer praise eternal;
Alleluia! Alleluia!

Jesus the health of the world, pour out your balm on our souls and the souls of all in pain or sorrow. Be the source of life for all people.
Invite the congregation to add their petitions and thanksgivings, followed by silence
To you we offer praise eternal;
Alleluia! Alleluia!

Purify us, O Lord, from all evil that we may rightly see you in the eternal light of your resurrection. By your victory, bring us from death to life eternal.
Silence
To you we offer praise eternal;
Alleluia! Alleluia!

Grace to you and peace from Jesus Christ, the firstborn of the dead. The Lord has acted; let us rejoice and be glad, saying, "You are our God; *and we thank you.*"

Almighty God, you have given your Church the ministry of reconciliation: grant that all who have been reborn into the fellowship of Christ's Body may show forth in their lives what they profess by their faith.
Silence
You are our God;
And we thank you.

Ruler of the kings of the earth, Lord Jesus, your word is a word of peace: speak forth salvation in a weary world.
Silence
You are our God;
And we thank you.

All you do, O Lord, is marvelous in our eyes: give us a respect for all you have made.
Invite the congregation to add their thanksgivings, followed by silence
You are our God;
And we thank you.

Mighty Savior, raise up faithful witnesses in our community, that our neighbors might come to know that you love them and have freed them from the power of sin.
Silence
You are our God;
And we thank you.

O Lord, you are good; your mercy endures forever: be the strength of the weak and the song of those who mourn.
Invite the congregation to add their petitions, followed by silence
You are our God;
And we thank you.

Alpha and Omega, you do not hand your beloved ones over to death, but promise life eternal to all those baptized into your Son: to you be glory and dominion forever.
Silence
You are our God;
And we thank you.

Brothers and sisters, give thanks to the One who clothes us with joy. The Lord is our helper and restorer; therefore, let us pray, "Hear, O Lord, *and have mercy upon us.*"

O God, you have chosen your Church to bring your name before all nations: give us hearts to feed your lambs and tend your sheep. Give us hearts to follow Jesus.
Silence
Hear, O Lord,
And have mercy upon us.

Lord Christ, we look for the day when all will live together in peace, when every voice will together sing this hymn: to the one seated on the throne and to the Lamb be blessing and honor and glory and might forever and ever!
Silence
Hear, O Lord,
And have mercy upon us.

Creator of the deep, protect and preserve our lakes, rivers, and oceans, and all creatures who live therein. May we be good stewards of the gift of water.
Invite the congregation to add their thanksgivings, followed by silence
Hear, O Lord,
And have mercy upon us.

Ancient of Days, we pray for the senior members of our community. Bless with patience and confidence those who rely on others for support, care, and transportation. Bless their caretakers with strength.
Silence
Hear, O Lord,
And have mercy upon us.

O Lord our God, restore to health those who cry out to you. Lift up the lowly. Turn wailing into joyful dancing.
Invite the congregation to add their petitions, followed by silence
Hear, O Lord,
And have mercy upon us.

Living God, you restore the life of those in the grave: may we, and all the dead, experience resurrection and life everlasting.
Silence
Hear, O Lord,
And have mercy upon us.

Salvation belongs to our God who is seated on the throne, and to the Lamb! The good shepherd is faithful and true; therefore, let us pray with confidence: "Father, keep us; *Jesus, lead us.*"

Good Shepherd, you know your sheep: give us the ears to hear you call our names and the strength to follow where you lead.
Silence
Father, keep us;
Jesus, lead us.

For those killed, injured, or traumatized because of human violence, we pray: God, wipe away every tear from their eyes. We pray again for an end to the violence. We pray again for peace.
Silence
Father, keep us;
Jesus, lead us.

Creator God, by the victory of your Son, turn the valleys of death into green pastures where living waters flow. Bless and renew your creation.
Invite the congregation to add their thanksgivings, followed by silence
Father, keep us;
Jesus, lead us.

O Lord, we pray for those who work for justice and peace in our community. Flood this city with goodness and mercy. Extinguish from our region the fear of evil.
Silence
Father, keep us;
Jesus, lead us.

Mighty God, we look for the day when hunger is no more, and thirst is no more. We look for the day when the souls of the downcast are revived, and the displaced find a home in your shelter. In this Easter season, we pray in faith for all those in need.
Invite the congregation to add their petitions, followed by silence
Father, keep us;
Jesus, lead us.

Good Shepherd, your gift is eternal life; those who belong to you never perish. Bring us, and those who have died, into your heavenly home where we may worship you forever and ever.
Silence
Father, keep us;
Jesus, lead us.

Easter 5C

Sisters and brothers, let us praise the name of the Lord! The promises of God are trustworthy and true, so let us pray, "Loving God, *make all things new.*"

Heavenly Father, your Son Jesus commands us to love one another as he loves us. Help us to do as he commands. Give your Church the will to seek and serve Christ in all persons.
Silence
Loving God,
Make all things new.

Gracious God, you blessed the world in your incarnation. Come and make your home with us. Establish your reign of peace on earth as in heaven.
Invite the congregation to add their thanksgivings, followed by silence
Loving God,
Make all things new.

Glorious Lord, you created the heavens and earth and all that is therein. At your command all things came into being. Give us ears to hear the praise coming forth from the worlds. May our voices join the song of creation.
Silence
Loving God,
Make all things new.

Grant, O God, that our city might become more like your heavenly city. Banish from our borders the pain of violence and addiction, abuse and hatred.
Silence
Loving God,
Make all things new.

Mighty God, wipe every tear from the eyes of your children. Come with healing. Come with strength. Come to your people.
Invite the congregation to add their petitions, followed by silence
Loving God,
Make all things new.

Alpha and Omega, we long for the day when you will make all things new. We long for the day when death will be no more, when mourning and crying and pain will be no more. We trust in the power of your love. Lead us in the way of everlasting life.
Silence
Loving God,
Make all things new.

Sisters and brothers, do not let your hearts be troubled, and do not let them be afraid. The God of peace has prepared for us such good things as surpass our understanding, so let us rejoice, saying, "Let the peoples praise you, O God; *let all the peoples praise you.*"

By the gift and power of the Holy Spirit, teach your Church to walk in the ways of Jesus. May the gospel be found in our minds, in our hearts, and on our lips.
Silence
Let the peoples praise you, O God;
Let all the peoples praise you.

Let the nations be glad and sing for joy, for you judge the peoples with equity and guide all the nations upon earth. We look for the day, O God, when all the peoples gather around your throne in praise and worship.
Invite the congregation to add their thanksgivings, followed by silence
Let the peoples praise you, O God;
Let all the peoples praise you.

O God from whom all good proceeds: bless the earth to bring forth her increase. Guide all your people to honor you by caring for your creation.
Silence
Let the peoples praise you, O God;
Let all the peoples praise you.

Give to our city, O God, your peace. Shine the light of your love on those places that are plagued by gangs and violence, hatred and sadness. Be merciful to us and bless us.
Silence
Let the peoples praise you, O God;
Let all the peoples praise you.

Almighty God, let your ways be known upon earth, your saving health among all nations. Give to the sick and suffering a taste of the water of life.
Invite the congregation to add their petitions, followed by silence
Let the peoples praise you, O God;
Let all the peoples praise you.

Grant us, O God, by your great mercy, entrance into your heavenly city where we might worship at your throne, see you face to face, and reign with you forever and ever.
Silence
Let the peoples praise you, O God;
Let all the peoples praise you.

Sisters and brothers, the grace of the Lord Jesus be with you and with all the saints. Our hope is found in the presence of the King of Glory, so let us appeal to the Lord, saying, "Amen. *Come, Lord Jesus!*"

We pray, Jesus, that your prayers might be answered: may your Church be one as you and the Father are one. And through our unity, may the whole world come to know your love.
Silence
Amen.
Come, Lord Jesus!

Most High, we eagerly await your return. We long for your reign of justice and righteousness. Now, even as we wait, deliver the innocent from the hands of the wicked; bless the truehearted with joyful gladness.
Silence
Amen.
Come, Lord Jesus!

O Lord, the heavens declare your righteousness. Give us eyes to see, ears to hear, lungs to breathe in your holy presence.
Invite the congregation to add their thanksgivings, followed by silence
Amen.
Come, Lord Jesus!

We pray, Lover of souls, for all those who are being exploited. We pray for those in bondage. We pray for those who suffer because of the greed of others.
Silence
Amen.
Come, Lord Jesus!

We pray for those who thirst for wholeness, for healing, for deliverance. We pray for all those who thirst. Give to the thirsty the gift of the water of life.
Invite the congregation to add their petitions, followed by silence
Amen.
Come, Lord Jesus!

Alpha and Omega, you bid your people, "Come!" May we, and all who have died, be with you, where you are, forever and ever.
Silence
Amen.
Come, Lord Jesus!

Friends, do not let your hearts be troubled, and do not let them be afraid. Our God is with us, and in us; therefore, let us pray: "Come, Spirit of Truth: *come, Holy Spirit.*"

Holy God, by your Spirit you gave birth to your Church: may our many members be the one Body of Christ in this world. And then lead us by your Holy Spirit in the ways of truth and love.
Silence
Come, Spirit of Truth:
Come, Holy Spirit.

Holy God, you gave your disciples the ability to speak in the languages of the people: may we also speak about your deeds of power throughout the world, that all may know of your salvation.
Silence
Come, Spirit of Truth:
Come, Holy Spirit.

Holy God, the earth is full of your creatures: may all who look to you be given food in due season. Open your hand in desolate places and fill the hungry with good things.
Invite the congregation to add thanksgivings, followed by silence
Come, Spirit of Truth:
Come, Holy Spirit.

Holy God, you poured out your Holy Spirit in your holy city Jerusalem: pour out your Spirit in our own city. Raise up prophets and dreamers; give us vision.
Silence
Come, Spirit of Truth:
Come, Holy Spirit.

Holy God, you give the gift of healing by your Spirit: bring healing and wholeness to all those on our hearts and minds this day. In your might and mercy, renew the face of the earth; bring renewal to those in need.
Invite the congregation to add their petitions, followed by silence
Come, Spirit of Truth:
Come, Holy Spirit.

Holy God, you adopt us as your children, joint heirs with your Christ. In your mercy, keep us and love us. May we, and all who have entered into your joy, rest in your presence forever.
Silence
Come, Spirit of Truth:
Come, Holy Spirit.

Trinity Sunday C

Sisters and brothers, we have been baptized into a holy mystery. As Christians, let us pray to God, saying, "Unity in Trinity, bend your ear. *Trinity in Unity, hear our prayer."*

Glory to you, Lord God of our forebears. Guide your Church into all truth by your Holy Spirit. Fill our hearts with hope so that we may fulfill the ministries to which we have been called with faith and boldness.
Silence
Unity in Trinity, bend your ear.
Trinity in Unity, hear our prayer.

Glory to you, Lord God. You delight in the human race. And so we trust that your heart breaks with the brokenhearted. Comfort all those who suffer because of natural disasters.
Unity in Trinity, bend your ear.
Trinity in Unity, hear our prayer.

Glory to you, Lord God. You established the heavens and marked out the foundations of the earth. Let all of creation praise you forever.
Invite the congregation to add their thanksgivings, followed by silence
Unity in Trinity, bend your ear.
Trinity in Unity, hear our prayer.

Glory to you, Lord God. By endurance you bring forth character in your people. We remember before you, O God, all those who have died in service to the people of this nation. For their courage and care, we give you thanks.
Silence
Unity in Trinity, bend your ear.
Trinity in Unity, hear our prayer.

Glory to you, Lord God. We pray for our loved ones because our hope is placed in you and hope placed in you, O God, does not disappoint. Bless and heal those for whom we pray.
Invite the congregation to add their petitions, followed by silence
Unity in Trinity, bend your ear.
Trinity in Unity, hear our prayer.

Glory to you, Father, Son, and Holy Spirit. Bring us at last to see you in your one and eternal glory.
Silence
Unity in Trinity, bend your ear.
Trinity in Unity, hear our prayer.

People of God, let us ascribe to the Lord the honor due God's name. Let us bring our prayers before God, saying, "Answer us, O Lord. *Answer your people.*"

Holy God, we marvel at the majesty and magnificence of your presence. Bless your Church with a new song. Let the whole earth be filled with the good news of salvation.
Silence
Answer us, O Lord.
Answer your people.

Mighty King, you judge the peoples with equity. May your rule of righteousness and truth overcome, even now, the dishonesty that plagues our lives.
Silence
Answer us, O Lord.
Answer your people.

The whole earth trembles before you, O God. Because of your presence the heavens rejoice, the earth is glad, the sea thunders and the fields are filled with joy, and we stand in awe and wonder. We give you thanks.
Invite the congregation to add their thanksgivings, followed by silence
Answer us, O Lord.
Answer your people.

Bless all those in the midst of transition, with your grace and peace. Put away from their lives all hurtful things and give them those things which are profitable for them, through Jesus our Lord.
Silence
Answer us, O Lord.
Answer your people.

Jesus, when the centurion petitioned you to heal his slave, you healed the slave. We pray in faith for those we love. May they know your healing power in their own lives.
Invite the congregation to add their petitions, followed by silence
Answer us, O Lord.
Answer your people.

God our Father, you raised from the dead your Son, Jesus Christ. By the same resurrection power, may we, with all the saints, share in his eternal life.
Silence
Answer us, O Lord.
Answer your people.

Proper 5C

Happy are they whose hope is in the Lord their God. Therefore, let us pray, saying, "Look favorably on your people, O God. *And hear our prayer.*"

Good God, you have called your Church into being through your grace: we pray that, because of our witness, the world may glorify you.
Silence
Look favorably on your people, O God.
And hear our prayer.

Lover of justice, you care for the stranger; you sustain the orphan and widow: frustrate the way of the wicked and give justice to those who are oppressed.
Silence
Look favorably on your people, O God.
And hear our prayer.

O God, from whom all good proceeds, who made heaven and earth, the seas, and all that is in them, we thank you for all that you have made and all that you are making still.
Invite the congregation to add their thanksgivings, followed by silence
Look favorably on your people, O God.
And hear our prayer.

Gracious God, we pray for all those who go forth into the world to share the good news of your love. Mercifully guide them in all their works.
Silence
Look favorably on your people, O God.
And hear our prayer.

Great Healer, you open the eyes of the blind; you lift up those who are bowed down; even death obeys your command: we cry out to you on behalf of the sick and the suffering, and all those we now name.
Invite the congregation to add their petitions, followed by silence
Look favorably on your people, O God.
And hear our prayer.

O Lord, you shall reign forever. By the resurrection of your Son, may we, and all the dead, live and reign with him, with you and with the Holy Spirit, forever and ever.
Silence
Look favorably on your people, O God.
And hear our prayer.

Brothers and sisters, hear the good news: Jesus loves us and gave himself for us. In faith we make our prayer to God, saying, "Give ear to our words, O Lord; *consider our meditation.*"

Keep, O Lord, your household the Church in your steadfast faith and love, that through your grace we may proclaim your truth with boldness, and minister your justice with compassion.
Silence
Give ear to our words, O Lord;
Consider our meditation.

O God, you take no pleasure in wickedness; you oppose the bloodthirsty and deceitful: frustrate the ways of those who oppress others. Defend the lowly. Be merciful to us all.
Silence
Give ear to our words, O Lord;
Consider our meditation.

Holy God, your Son Jesus ministered in the cities and in the villages: bless us in our diverse locations to spread the good news of your coming Kingdom to all people.
Silence
Give ear to our words, O Lord;
Consider our meditation.

Raise up good fathers, O God, who will model for their children the love of Jesus—loving others as he loves us. Lead them in righteousness and sustain them by your faithfulness.
Invite the congregation to add their thanksgivings, followed by silence
Give ear to our words, O Lord;
Consider our meditation.

In the name of Jesus we pray for the healing and restoration of those who are sick or suffering, those who are in sorrow or pain.
Invite the congregation to add their petitions, followed by silence
Give ear to our words, O Lord;
Consider our meditation.

Holy God, you are the God of the living and the dead: we pray that those who have been crucified with Christ will also share in his resurrection.
Silence
Give ear to our words, O Lord;
Consider our meditation.

Proper 7C

There is no longer Jew or Greek, there is no longer slave or free, there is no longer male or female; for all of us are one in Christ Jesus. Let us pray as one body, saying, "We put our trust in you, O God; *hear us; answer us; and send us forth.*"

Send out your light and your truth that they may lead your people into the joy and gladness we experience at your altar. Send us out to shine our light and share our joy.
Silence
We put our trust in you, O God;
Hear us; answer us; and send us forth.

God our strength, remember those who feel forgotten, be the salvation for those who are being oppressed. Defend the cause of the innocent. Deliver the world from wickedness.
Silence
We put our trust in you, O God;
Hear us; answer us; and send us forth.

You, O Lord, grant your loving-kindness in the daytime, the night is filled with your songs: we thank you for blessing your creation with your presence in all times and all seasons.
Invite the congregation to add their thanksgivings, followed by silence
We put our trust in you, O God;
Hear us; answer us; and send us forth.

Lord Jesus, break the chains of those held in bondage. Restore those forgotten by society. May all prisoners and captives, by the power of your love and mercy, have their dignity renewed.
Silence
We put our trust in you, O God;
Hear us; answer us; and send us forth.

We pray for those weighed down by heavy souls. We pray for those who feel like they are in over their heads; for the disquieted and for the ill.
Invite the congregation to add their petitions, followed by silence
We put our trust in you, O God;
Hear us; answer us; and send us forth.

O God, in Christ Jesus you have made us your children. We pray for the dying and the dead. Bring them into your heavenly dwelling where they may be at home with you forever.
Silence
We put our trust in you, O God;
Hear us; answer us; and send us forth.

If we live by the Spirit, brothers and sisters, let us also be guided by the Spirit. And, guided by the Spirit, let us lift our prayers to the Lord, saying, "We cry aloud to you; *O God, hear us.*"

We give you thanks, O God, that for freedom Christ has set us free. Though at times it challenges our patience, we also give you thanks for the freedom, through love, to become servants of one another.
Silence
We cry aloud to you;
O God, hear us.

Gracious God, give us the will and the strength to prepare the way for your Kingdom to come. May love heal our factions and peace overcome strife.
Silence
We cry aloud to you; .
O God, hear us.

Your paths are in the great waters, mighty Redeemer. We thank you that by the waters of baptism you have made us members of your household.
Invite the congregation to add their thanksgivings, followed by silence
We cry aloud to you;
O God, hear us.

Lord Jesus, you rebuked your disciples James and John when they desired the destruction of others. Instill in us gentleness and self-control that we might learn to love even those with whom we strongly disagree.
Silence
We cry aloud to you;
O God, hear us.

You are the God who works wonders. We offer to you our sincere prayers for our hurting loved ones. Work wonders in their hearts and lives, we pray.
Invite the congregation to add their petitions, followed by silence
We cry aloud to you;
O God, hear us.

By your strength, O God, you redeem your people. Lead us by your Spirit and make us fit for your heavenly Kingdom.
Silence
We cry aloud to you;
O God, hear us.

Friends, let us not grow weary in doing what is right. Let us appeal to God, who is our Strength, praying, "Hear, O Lord, *and have mercy upon us.*"

We ask you, O Lord of the harvest, to send out laborers into your harvest. Grant us the grace of your Holy Spirit, that your Church might freely proclaim, in word and deed, the good news of your Kingdom.
Silence
Hear, O Lord,
And have mercy upon us.

Give us, O God, the opportunity and the will to work for the good of all. Give us hearts for the people you love.
Silence
Hear, O Lord,
And have mercy upon us.

We thank you, Almighty God, for the gift of water. In it Naaman was cleansed from his disease. By it the whole earth is refreshed. Through it we are reborn by the Holy Spirit.
Silence
Hear, O Lord,
And have mercy upon us.

Gracious God, we thank you for our freedom. May we use it to bear one another's burdens and to live in peace.
Invite the congregation to add their thanksgivings, followed by silence
Hear, O Lord,
And have mercy upon us.

O Lord, our helper, you turn wailing into dancing; you dress your children in joy. We pray that you would restore to health all those who cry out to you.
Invite the congregation to add their petitions, followed by silence
Hear, O Lord,
And have mercy upon us.

Holy God, it is our joy that you write our names in heaven. In the fullness of time, raise us, with all the saints, to eternal life that we might give you thanks forever.
Silence
Hear, O Lord,
And have mercy upon us.

Brothers and sisters, grace to you and peace from God our Father. Let us pray in hope, trusting that God receives our prayers, saying, "Lord, in your mercy, *hear our prayer.*"

Grant to your Church, O God, understanding, that we may know your will for us, and also may have the grace and power faithfully to accomplish those things to which you call us.
Silence
Lord, in your mercy,
Hear our prayer.

Arise, O God, and rule the earth. Save the weak and the orphan; defend the humble and the needy; deliver them from the power of the wicked.
Silence
Lord, in your mercy,
Hear our prayer.

Bless those who tend to herds. Bless those who dress trees. Bless those who care for the earth. Bless those who work so that we might enjoy the fruits of their labor.
Invite the congregation to add their thanksgivings, followed by silence
Lord, in your mercy,
Hear our prayer.

We pray, O Lord, that we might be good neighbors. Increase in our hearts compassion for the vulnerable in our own city and in the surrounding communities.
Silence
Lord, in your mercy,
Hear our prayer.

Gracious God, show mercy to those who are suffering. Renew them; make them strong with all the strength that comes from your glorious power.
Invite the congregation to add their petitions, followed by silence
Lord, in your mercy,
Hear our prayer.

We give you thanks, O God. You have enabled us to share in the inheritance of the saints in the light. Heavenly Parent, you have rescued us from the power of darkness and transferred us into the kingdom of your beloved Son, in whom we have redemption.
Silence
Lord, in your mercy,
Hear our prayer.

Friends, let us come before the Lord in prayerful reverence saying, "God of Glory, *reveal yourself to us.*"

Grant, Almighty God, that we your Church, the body of your Son in this world, may present ourselves holy and blameless and irreproachable before you.
Silence
God of Glory,
Reveal yourself to us.

Guide the people of this land, and of all the nations, in the ways of justice and peace; that we may generously welcome both friend and stranger.
Silence
God of Glory,
Reveal yourself to us.

Lord God, open our hearts. Inspire us to be generous with all we have and all we are. May our own generosity reflect the generosity that you show us.
Invite the congregation to add their prayers of thanksgiving, followed by silence
God of Glory,
Reveal yourself to us.

Bless all those we have long loved and those we are learning to love and those who are yet strangers in our lives; grant that we may honor the Christ in them, that our kindness may refresh and bless all we meet.
Silence
God of Glory,
Reveal yourself to us.

Comfort and heal all those who suffer any affliction; give them strength and courage in their troubles, and remind them of the hope of glory they find in Christ.
Invite the congregation to add their petitions, followed by silence
God of Glory,
Reveal yourself to us.

We commend to your mercy all who have died, that they may be eternally reconciled to you through Jesus Christ; and we pray that we may forever dwell with Mary and Martha and all your faithful servants in your blessed presence.
Silence
God of Glory,
Reveal yourself to us.

Brothers and sisters, God's salvation is very near. Reverently and fearfully, let us pray to the Lord, saying, *"We call to you, O God; answer us."*

Make your Church alive, O God, together with your risen Christ. Forgive our trespasses, erase all records that stand against us and save us from the time of trial.
Silence
We call to you, O God;
Answer us.

By your victory on the cross, Lord Christ, you have triumphed over all things. We pray that we may witness your kingdom come, your will be done, on earth as in heaven.
Silence
We call to you, O God,
Answer us.

Help us to be good stewards of your creation, that each and every person will be given their daily bread.
Invite the congregation to add their prayers of thanksgiving, followed by silence
We call to you, O God,
Answer us.

We pray, God our protector, for all those with uncertain futures. Make your good purpose known, O God, in their lives. May they know that you, Father, give good gifts to your children.
Silence
We call to you, O God,
Answer us.

Comfort and heal all those who are in pain or sorrow or any kind of trouble. Do not abandon the works of your hands. Be found, gracious God, by all those who search for you.
Invite the congregation to add their petitions, followed by silence
We call to you, O God,
Answer us.

We commend to your mercy all who have died. And, we thank you, Gracious God, that all who are buried with Christ in baptism shall also experience the power of his resurrection.
Silence
We call to you, O God,
Answer us.

Sisters and brothers, children of God, let us come before the Most High with humility, saying, "Great and holy God, *incline your ear to us.*"

Set our minds on things divine, O God, that your Church may guard itself against the love of earthly things and instead be rich towards you.
Silence
Great and holy God,
Incline your ear to us.

May all who dwell in the world, those of both high degree and low, incline their hearts to wisdom and meditate on understanding.
Silence
Great and holy God,
Incline your ear to us.

Give us grace to be wise and generous stewards, O God. Open our eyes to see your abundance and our reliance.
Invite the congregation to add prayers of thanksgiving, followed by silence
Great and holy God,
Incline your ear to us.

Bless all those to whom we are connected. May we value our relationships more than our possessions. May we realize that in Christ all human distinctions cease to matter. We pray for justice and peace.
Silence
Great and holy God,
Incline your ear to us.

Comfort and heal all those who are in pain or sorrow or any kind of trouble. May we, who have known sorrow, pain and trouble, show them mercy and compassion and remind them of the hope we have in Christ.
Invite the congregation to add intercessions, followed by silence
Great and holy God,
Incline your ear to us.

We acknowledge our mortality before you, Everlasting God, and we rejoice in the hope of being raised with your Christ. We remember before you the lives of our forebears; may they find, in you, rest from their labors.
Silence
Great and holy God,
Incline your ear to us.

Do not be afraid, children of Abraham; God, your God, is your shield. So, let us approach our God, saying, "Let your loving-kindness, O Lord, be upon us; *we put our trust in you.*"

As your Church, we confess that we are strangers seeking a homeland. Do not be ashamed to call yourself our God and make us worthy of that heavenly city you have prepared for us.
Silence
Let your loving-kindness, O Lord, be upon us;
We put our trust in you.

Mighty God, you behold all of the people in the world. May all tribes and nations come to understand that our strength is not found in violence or weapons but in the power of your love.
Silence
Let your loving-kindness, O Lord, be upon us;
We put our trust in you.

Creator God, you are the one who made the stars of heaven and the sand by the seashore. We bless and honor you for the gifts of creation.
Invite the congregation to add their prayers of thanksgiving, followed by silence
Let your loving-kindness, O Lord, be upon us;
We put our trust in you.

Defend the orphans, O God; rescue the oppressed; show compassion to those who feel lonely or isolated. And let the heavens declare the rightness of your cause.
Silence
Let your loving-kindness, O Lord, be upon us;
We put our trust in you.

Comfort and heal the sick and the sorrowful. May they know that you are their help and shield. Deliver them from all fear and help them to trust in your righteousness.
Invite the congregation to add their petitions, followed by silence
Let your loving-kindness, O Lord, be upon us;
We put our trust in you.

Indeed, by faith our ancestors received approval. We praise you, God, that those who have died are welcomed home, where they will dwell with all men and women of faith in the city you have prepared for them.
Silence
Let your loving-kindness, O Lord, be upon us;
We put our trust in you.

Surrounded by so great a cloud of witnesses, and guided by the perfecter of our faith, let us bring our prayers before God, saying, "Behold your children, *and restore us, O God of hosts.*"

Inspire in your Church the faithfulness of the saints. Following in their footsteps, may we lay aside every weight and the sin that clings so closely, and run with perseverance the race that is set before us.
Silence
Behold your children,
And restore us, O God of hosts.

Almighty Judge, you rule the earth with your justice and mercy. Save the weak and the orphan; defend the humble and the needy; rescue the weak and the poor; forgive us when we fail to be merciful.
Silence
Behold your children,
And restore us, O God of hosts.

By your Word, O God, you created the heavens and the earth. By your generosity you continue to cause growth. In your faithfulness you clothe, protect, and sustain your children. We honor you for your creativity and your provision.
Invite the congregation to add their prayers of thanksgiving, followed by silence
Behold your children,
And restore us, O God of hosts.

Bless all those who have taught us to live faithfully. May our lives also witness to your Son Jesus, the pioneer and perfecter of our faith.
Silence
Behold your children,
And restore us, O God of hosts.

We pray for all who suffer and struggle. May they take comfort in knowing that you are not a God who is far off but you are very near us, even filling heaven and earth.
Invite the congregation to add their petitions, followed by silence
Behold your children,
And restore us, O God of hosts.

We praise you for all the saints, both famous and obscure, who surround us with their prayers, their encouragement and their strength. Make us ever mindful of the great company that makes with us our earthly pilgrimage.
Silence
Behold your children,
And restore us, O God of hosts.

Sisters and brothers, the Lord is full of compassion and mercy. Let us then pray to the Lord, saying, *"You, O God, are our hope; incline your ear to us."*

O Lord, may your Church take delight in you above all else. Fill our hearts with joy and gladness as we worship in your presence. May we faithfully keep the feast.
Invite the congregation to add their thanksgivings, followed by silence
You, O God, are our hope;
Incline your ear to us.

Give to the leaders of nations, O Lord, compassion for the hungry; satisfy the needs of the afflicted. May we, satisfied with good things, show mercy to the poor and oppressed.
Silence
You, O God, are our hope;
Incline your ear to us.

God, you are a consuming fire. Your light rises in the darkness and our gloom becomes like the noonday. Continue to make yourself known to us in your creation—in the stars of the night and the new light of the morning.
Silence
You, O God, are our hope;
Incline your ear to us.

You call us, O God, into a great community of believers: to join with angels and saints, with those you have made righteous, and with your Son Jesus, the mediator of the new covenant. We pray for our fellow Christians around the world, especially those facing persecution. Protect and strengthen them. Have mercy, Lord.
Silence
You, O God, are our hope;
Incline your ear to us.

We pray for the healing of those who are spiritually and physically broken. May all who are troubled by the power of evil find freedom in the hands of your Son.
Invite the congregation to add their petitions, followed by silence
You, O God, are our hope;
Incline your ear to us.

O God, you redeem life from the grave through the resurrection of Christ. We pray for those who have died in hope; may they eternally be satisfied with good things.
Silence
You, O God, are our hope;
Incline your ear to us.

Brothers and sisters, God will never leave us or forsake us. Let us humbly appeal to our faithful God, saying, "We offer to you, O God, a sacrifice of praise; *we offer the fruit of our lips."*

We pray for our leaders, those who speak your word to us, especially our Bishop and our Priest. May your whole Church listen for your voice and obey your words.
Invite the congregation to add their thanksgivings, followed by silence
We offer to you, O God, a sacrifice of praise;
We offer the fruit of our lips.

O God, you exalt the humble and humble the exalted. We pray that the leaders of the nations will serve their people in humility and manage their affairs with justice. May the poor and lowly be treated with respect and shown mercy.
Silence
We offer to you, O God, a sacrifice of praise;
We offer the fruit of our lips.

You have created a beautiful planet, full of wondrous creatures and magnificent works. Open our eyes to see your hand at work in the world about us.
Silence
We offer to you, O God, a sacrifice of praise;
We offer the fruit of our lips.

We pray for all laborers: for those who work, that they might be fulfilled; for those in need of work, that they might find meaningful employment; for those who are struggling to make ends meet, that they might receive a fair wage for their labors. In labor and in rest, be glorified by all we do.
Silence
We offer to you, O God, a sacrifice of praise;
We offer the fruit of our lips.

We pray for the strength to do your will. May we boldly and compassionately welcome the poor, the crippled, the lame, and the blind. May all of us know you as God our helper.
Invite the congregation to add their petitions, followed by silence
We offer to you, O God, a sacrifice of praise;
We offer the fruit of our lips.

O God you invite those who have died to feast at your heavenly banquet. We take great hope in the promise that not even death will cause you to leave us or forsake us.
Silence
We offer to you, O God, a sacrifice of praise;
We offer the fruit of our lips.

Brothers and sisters, grace to you and peace from God our Father and the Lord Jesus Christ. Let us pray to the Lord, saying, "Christ, in your mercy, *refresh our hearts.*"

We remember in our prayers all the leaders of your Church. May they, by their love and witness, inspire your children to greater joy and encouragement.
Silence
Christ, in your mercy,
Refresh our hearts.

We remember in our prayers the leaders of the nations. May they choose ways of life and not paths of death. Deliver the nations of the world from violence and war. Set our feet on the way of peace.
Silence
Christ, in your mercy,
Refresh our hearts.

We remember in our prayers all of your creation. May we protect the trees, the streams and the fruits of the earth. Forgive us when our choices cause death where you intend life. May we ever celebrate the life-giving aspects of your creation.
Invite the congregation to add their thanksgivings, followed by silence
Christ, in your mercy,
Refresh our hearts.

We remember in our prayers this congregation. We ask you to bless our ministries, especially today the choir, the Sunday School and the acolytes. May we encourage each other to delight in you. Let us appeal to each other on the basis of love and always remember our sisters and brothers in prayer.
Silence
Christ, in your mercy,
Refresh our hearts.

We remember in our prayers all those who are in pain. Heal their bodies, their spirits, and their souls. Bless all with life and prosperity.
Invite the congregation to add their petitions, followed by silence
Christ, in your mercy,
Refresh our hearts.

We remember in our prayers all those who have died. May all who have carried the cross in the way of Christ also be raised with him to new life.
Silence
Christ, in your mercy,
Refresh our hearts.

Brothers and sisters, God is our refuge. Let us implore the Lord our God praying, "Create in me a clean heart, O God, *and renew a right spirit within me."*

We pray for the leaders of the Church. Make them worthy examples to those who would come to believe in Christ for eternal life. May the Church place its hope in you, O God, and not in human wisdom.
Silence
Create in me a clean heart, O God,
And renew a right spirit within me.

We pray for the leaders of the nations. May they show mercy and advocate for the rights of the people. May they, like Moses, seek the greater good rather than self-interest.
Silence
Create in me a clean heart, O God,
And renew a right spirit within me.

We thank you for all you created. We thank you that your Son Jesus Christ rejoiced in your creation, seeing the Kingdom of God even in a field of sheep. Open our eyes and our hearts.
Invite the congregation to add their thanksgivings, followed by silence
Create in me a clean heart, O God,
And renew a right spirit within me.

We pray for those who are lost, that they might be found. We pray for those who are sure they are not lost; we ask that you find them too. And we thank you that in your mercy you seek until you find.
Silence
Create in me a clean heart, O God,
And renew a right spirit within me.

We pray for the sick, the anxious and the sorrowful. Make them hear of joy and gladness, that broken bodies and broken spirits may rejoice.
Invite the congregation to add their petitions, followed by silence
Create in me a clean heart, O God,
And renew a right spirit within me.

We trust to your mercy, O God, all who have died. May they rest eternally in your peace. To the King of the ages, immortal, invisible, the only God, our God, be honor and glory forever and ever.
Silence
Create in me a clean heart, O God,
And renew a right spirit within me.

Brothers and sisters, I urge that supplications, prayers, intercessions, and thanksgivings be made for everyone. Let us pray, saying, *"We bless your name, O Lord, from this time forth forevermore."*

We make our prayers for all Church leaders. May all those called to be heralds and apostles serve you, the Church, and the world in all godliness and dignity.
Invite the congregation to add their thanksgivings, followed by silence
We bless your name, O Lord,
From this time forth forevermore.

We make our prayers for kings and all who are in high positions. May they make laws that protect the poor and promote justice. Set their hearts on truth.
Silence
We bless your name, O Lord,
From this time forth forevermore.

O God you created the heavens and the earth. Give us the courage and diligence to care for your creation. Grant us to live at peace and harmony with all the works of your hands.
Silence
We bless your name, O Lord,
From this time forth forevermore.

God, we have had more than enough of violence and bloodshed. So let your compassion be swift to meet us. Help us, O God our Savior, for the glory of your name; deliver us and forgive us our sins, for your name's sake.
Silence
We bless your name, O Lord,
From this time forth forevermore.

We pray for the poor and the needy. We thank you that you remember even those we too often ignore and disregard. Give us grace to proclaim to every person the good news of your love and faithfulness.
Invite the congregation to add their petitions, followed by silence
We bless your name, O Lord,
From this time forth forevermore.

We make our prayers for all who have died. We thank you that you sent Christ Jesus to humankind, that through him everyone might come to the knowledge of your eternal salvation.
Silence
We bless your name, O Lord,
From this time forth forevermore.

Sisters and brothers, let us set our hope on God and pray to our God, saying, "God, our refuge and stronghold, *we put our trust in you.*"

We pray for your one holy, catholic, and apostolic Church. May we and your whole Church pursue righteousness, godliness, faith, love, endurance, and gentleness.
Silence
God, our refuge and stronghold,
We put our trust in you.

We pray for the leaders of this and every nation. Remind us that they are fallible human beings, fellow children of the earth. May they put their trust in you, even as we trust in you for our help.
Silence
God, our refuge and stronghold,
We put our trust in you.

Creating God, you made heaven and earth, the seas, and all that is in them. Make us good stewards of your bounty, that there may be food enough for all who hunger.
Invite the congregation to add their thanksgivings, followed by silence
God, our refuge and stronghold,
We put our trust in you.

Open our eyes to see the poor at our gates. Give us compassion for those suffering in our community. You, O Lord, care for the stranger; you sustain the orphan and widow. May our work reflect your heart.
Silence
God, our refuge and stronghold,
We put our trust in you.

We pray for the hungry, the sick and the dying. Grant comfort and mercy to those who now experience evil things.
Invite the congregation to add their petitions, followed by silence
God, our refuge and stronghold,
We put our trust in you.

We pray for those who have died. May all the departed find new life in the presence of their God, the one who alone has immortality and dwells in unapproachable light.
Silence
God, our refuge and stronghold,
We put our trust in you.

Sisters and brothers, grace, mercy, and peace from God our Parent and Christ Jesus our Lord. Let us pray together, saying, "Lord, you are our portion, *therefore will we hope in you."*

Give to your Church, O Lord, the strength to hold to sound teaching, the grace to treasure the faith and love that are in Christ Jesus, and the help of the Holy Spirit to please you in all things.
Silence
Lord, you are our portion,
Therefore will we hope in you.

Liberate the nations and kingdoms of this world from the ways of violence and war. Have mercy on the victims of war—especially those who are considered collateral damage—and on those who perpetrate violence that they might be converted to the ways of love.
Silence
Lord, you are our portion,
Therefore will we hope in you.

Pour upon us the abundance of your mercy, O God. Bless the earth and its creatures. May we be good and worthy stewards.
Invite the congregation to add their thanksgivings, followed by silence
Lord, you are our portion,
Therefore will we hope in you.

Great Governor, your mercies are new every morning: We pray today for all those who are negatively affected by our political processes and partisan divisions. We pray that you would inspire our leaders to act selflessly and with generosity.
Silence
Lord, you are our portion,
Therefore will we hope in you.

Everlasting God, you are always more ready to hear than we to pray, and to give more that we either desire or deserve: through your Son Jesus, comfort, heal and deliver your people, especially those we name now.
Invite the congregation to add their petitions, followed by silence
Lord, you are our portion,
Therefore will we hope in you.

Loving God, in your Christ you abolished death and brought life and immortality to light through the gospel: bless the dying and dead, and give to us all eternal life.
Silence
Lord, you are our portion,
Therefore will we hope in you.

Great are the deeds of the Lord! Sisters and brothers, let us pray, saying, "Christ, hear our prayer! *Jesus, have mercy on us!*"

May your Church be faithful, even as you are faithful. May we and your whole Church unashamedly work to further the gospel. May we overcome whatever apathy or distraction might threaten our witness.
Silence
Christ, hear our prayer!
Jesus, have mercy on us!

May the nations of the world seek wisdom and truth. May people, rich and poor, powerful and weak, find in you the source of healing and wholeness.
Invite the congregation to add their thanksgivings, followed by silence
Christ, hear our prayer!
Jesus, have mercy on us!

May we protect and guard the created order. May we recognize the majesty and splendor of all you have made. May we remember that healthy waters, sky, and land make us healthier people.
Silence
Christ, hear our prayer!
Jesus, have mercy on us!

May we be ever compassionate towards those who are pushed into the margins of our society. Give us open hearts that welcome and open hands that touch. Teach us a love that crosses boundaries and borders.
Silence
Christ, hear our prayer!
Jesus, have mercy on us!

May the sick and suffering know in their bodies and minds your healing power. You desire to make men and women clean of disease and stigma; make your grace known.
Invite the congregation to add their petitions, followed by silence
Christ, hear our prayer!
Jesus, have mercy on us!

May those who have died know the salvation found in you, Christ Jesus. Preserve the living in the enduring hope that, just as we are baptized into your death, so will we also live with you forever.
Silence
Christ, hear our prayer!
Jesus, have mercy on us!

Brothers and sisters, our help comes from the Lord, the maker of heaven and earth. And yet, we can pray, saying, "Put your word within us, O God; *write it on our hearts.*"

We pray, O God, for the Church and its leaders. May we proclaim the truth and share the Good News. Give your Church grace that each member may carry out his or her ministry fully.
Invite the congregation to offer their thanksgivings, followed by silence
Put your word within us, O God;
Write it on our hearts.

We pray, O God, for all those who interpret and establish laws, especially judges. Give our leaders wisdom equal to their responsibilities, that they may serve the common good and promote justice throughout the world.
Silence
Put your word within us, O God;
Write it on our hearts.

We pray, O God, for all of creation. In the beauty of hills and streams, we glimpse your majesty. In the wonder of sun and moon, we glimpse your power. May we be responsible in our care and protection of all you have given us.
Silence
Put your word within us, O God;
Write it on our hearts.

We pray, O God, for the people of our community. May those who cry out for justice, see justice. May those who search for truth, find truth. May those who fear for their own safety, find their comfort and security in you.
Silence
Put your word within us, O God;
Write it on our hearts.

We pray, O God, for the sick and the sorrowful. May those who call upon you for healing also find you to be their faithful healer.
Invite the congregation to add their petitions, followed by silence
Put your word within us, O God;
Write it on our hearts.

We pray, O God, for all who have died. May all those justified by your Son, Christ Jesus, be judged by him as faithful and good.
Silence
Put your word within us, O God;
Write it on our hearts.

Proper 25C

Happy are the people whose strength is in the Lord! Let us come humbly before the Most High, praying, "God be merciful, *And hear our prayer.*"

Lord, be merciful to your Church. Forgive us our pride and the times we obscure your mercy. Give us humility that we may generously give to you as you have given to us.
Silence
God be merciful,
And hear our prayer.

Lord, be merciful to our nation. Forgive us our pride and the times we have gloried in our own accomplishments. Give us humility that we may generously care for the orphans, the widows, and all those in need.
Silence
God be merciful,
And hear our prayer.

Lord, be merciful to us, those called to care for your creation. Forgive us our pride and the times we have polluted the springs and pools of water with which you have blessed us. Give us humility that we may generously deal with all of your creation.
Silence
God be merciful,
And hear our prayer.

Lord, be merciful to the residents of our community. Forgive us our pride and the times we fail to trust that you stand by us and give us the strength we need. Give us humility that we may generously address the challenges that face us.
Silence
God be merciful,
And hear our prayer.

Lord, be merciful to all those with broken hearts, bodies, and souls. Forgive us our pride and the times we have exalted ourselves above your suffering servants. Give us humility that we may generously love all your people.
Invite the congregation to add their petitions and thanksgivings, followed by silence
God be merciful,
And hear our prayer.

Lord, be merciful to all who have died. Accept them into the glorious company of the communion of saints. Make for them a home in your dwelling forever.
Silence
God be merciful,
And hear our prayer.

O Lord, we come before you asking that you listen to us and cleanse us from our sins. Let us pray to God, saying, "O God make us worthy of your call, *that the name of Jesus may be glorified in us."*

O God, we offer back to you the Church. May we be steadfast in faith and fervent in prayer. May we worship you with clean hands and pure hearts.
Silence
O God, make us worthy of your call,
That the name of Jesus may be glorified in us.

O God, we offer back to you our nation. Compel us to do good and seek justice. Guide our decision-making that we may be a people who do your will.
Silence
O God, make us worthy of your call,
That the name of Jesus may be glorified in us.

O God, we offer back to you those things you have created for our survival and pleasure. May we be faithful stewards of all we have. May our gifts be used to glorify your Son, support your Church, and bless the world.
Silence
O God, make us worthy of your call,
That the name of Jesus may be glorified in us.

O God, we offer back to you our city. Establish the city on the strong foundation of love and justice.
Silence
O God, make us worthy of your call,
That the name of Jesus may be glorified in us.

O God, we offer back to you all those on our hearts and minds this day. May they come to know you as the God of their salvation. By your grace preserve them in trouble and surround them with shouts of deliverance.
Invite the congregation to add their petitions and thanksgivings, followed by silence
O God make us worthy of your call,
That the name of Jesus may be glorified in us.

O God, we offer back to you all who have died. We praise you for their faith and witness. And we ask that they experience the fullness of grace and peace in your heavenly home.
Silence
O God, make us worthy of your call,
That the name of Jesus may be glorified in us.

All Saints' Day C (or the Sunday closest)

The Lord takes great pleasure in us. God cares for us and hears our prayers. So let us pray: "We offer our prayers; *Our hope is set on you, O Christ.*"

Bless your Church, O Lord. Increase our faith in you. Increase our love for one another. Increase in us a spirit of wisdom.
Silence
We offer our prayers;
Our hope is set on you, O Christ.

Bless the human family, O Lord. Bless the poor. Bless the hungry. Bless those who now weep.
Silence
We offer our prayers;
Our hope is set on you, O Christ.

Bless this good creation, O Lord. All things were made through you and by your resurrection they are given new life. We thank you that you are already making all things new.
Invite the congregation to add thanksgivings, followed by Silence
We offer our prayers;
Our hope is set on you, O Christ.

Bless this city, O Lord. May we be known as a generous people—doing to our neighbors as we would have them do to us.
Silence
We offer our prayers;
Our hope is set on you, O Christ.

Bless those in need, O Lord. You adorn the poor with victory; you fill those who are hungry. Make happy those for whom we pray.
Invite the congregation to add their petitions, followed by Silence
We offer our prayers;
Our hope is set on you, O Christ.

Bless the saints who now rest from their labors, O Lord. Give to them the kingdom of God as a possession—for ever and ever.
Silence
We offer our prayers;
Our hope is set on you, O Christ.

Brothers and sisters, the Lord is near to those who call. So let us offer our prayers, saying, "We call upon you, O God, *for you will answer us.*"

Generous God, we pray for the Church. We pray that you comfort and strengthen us in every good work and deed. Give us courage in uncertain times.
Silence
We call upon you, O God,
For you will answer us.

O Lord, you are righteous in all your ways. Where, in the world, the innocent cry out for justice, hear their cries and help them.
Silence
We call upon you, O God,
For you will answer us.

Make us quick to ponder the glorious splendor of your majesty. Open our eyes, great Creator, to all your marvelous works.
Invite the congregation to add their thanksgivings, followed by silence
We call upon you, O God,
For you will answer us.

Holy God, vindicator of the innocent, we ask you to bless and keep all those who offer their time and services and lives to defend the helpless and the threatened. May we live to see a day when violence and war are no more.
Silence
We call upon you, O God,
For you will answer us.

Great God, those with whom your Spirit abides need not fear. Hide those who are distraught and those who are afraid under the shadow of your wings. Through grace, give to your saints eternal comfort and good hope.
Invite the congregation to add their petitions, followed by silence
We call upon you, O God,
For you will answer us.

God of the living, in you all are alive. May those who now rest in peace, one day rise to behold you face to face.
Silence
We call upon you, O God,
For you will answer us.

Brothers and sisters, do not be weary in doing what is right. It is right to give God thanks and praise; therefore, let us say, "Sing to the Lord a new song: *O God, you have done marvelous things!"*

O God, remember your mercy and faithfulness to your Church. Give us your words and your wisdom. May we have the strength to bear the name of Jesus in all circumstances.
Silence
Sing to the Lord a new song:
O God, you have done marvelous things!

O God, remember your mercy and faithfulness to this nation. Save us from arrogance and self-reliance. Grant us to be a nation that favors peace over war, life rather than death.
Silence
Sing to the Lord a new song:
O God, you have done marvelous things!

O God, remember your mercy and faithfulness to all of creation. May the seas and their creatures noisily praise you; may the rivers clap their hands and the hills ring out with joy before you, their Creator.
Silence
Sing to the Lord a new song:
O God, you have done marvelous things!

O God, remember your mercy and faithfulness to our city. We pray that there may be work enough for all our citizens, that they might earn a living that promotes dignity and health.
Silence
Sing to the Lord a new song:
O God, you have done marvelous things!

O God, remember your mercy and faithfulness to all your children, especially those who are sick and suffering. Come to them, Lover of Souls, with healing in your wings.
Invite the congregation to add their petitions and thanksgivings, followed by silence
Sing to the Lord a new song:
O God, you have done marvelous things!

O God, remember your mercy and faithfulness to all who have died. Bless them for their endurance. May they forever rest in that land where the sound of weeping is heard no more.
Silence
Sing to the Lord a new song:
O God, you have done marvelous things!

Sisters and brothers, God has raised up for us a righteous king: Jesus our Christ. Let us lift our prayers to him, saying, "We praise you, Christ the King; *you have come to your people and set us free!*"

King Jesus, remember your body, the Church. You have rescued us from the power of darkness and have transferred us into your kingdom. Make us strong with all the strength that comes from your glorious power.
Silence
We praise you, Christ the King;
You have come to your people and set us free!

King Jesus, remember this nation. Guide our feet into the way of peace. Raise up leaders who govern their people wisely and justly.
Silence
We praise you, Christ the King;
You have come to your people and set us free!

King Jesus, all things in heaven and on earth are created through you and for you. May we who care for your creation do so with all due respect.
Silence
We praise you, Christ the King;
You have come to your people and set us free!

King Jesus, remember this region in which we live and work and worship. Drive far from us all fear and dismay. Rescue the missing; find the lost. May all of your children live in safety.
Silence
We praise you, Christ the King;
You have come to your people and set us free!

King Jesus, you know intimately the experience of pain and suffering in your own body. May all those suffering know that you are with them in their pain.
Invite the congregation to add their petitions and thanksgivings, followed by silence
We praise you, Christ the King;
You have come to your people and set us free!

King Jesus, accept those who have died into your kingdom. Give all the departed peace through the blood of your cross and, in the fullness of time, raise them to newness of life.
Silence
We praise you, Christ the King;
You have come to your people and set us free!

CONCLUDING COLLECTS

Holy Parent, in your tenderness and compassion, hear our prayers. May they be to you as a precious offering from the treasure of our hearts. We present them to you because you are faithful and your love endures forever and ever. AMEN.

Holy and Merciful God, open your ears to our call; listen to the cries of our hearts. Accept our prayers and answer them according to your good and perfect will. In the name of Jesus, the Lord of glory, we pray. AMEN.

Show your goodness, O Lord, and hear our prayers. Look past our selfish desires and remember your own faithfulness. In your great compassion, consider our petitions and in your mercy do in our lives that which is truly good. We pray in the name of your Son, who with you and the Holy Spirit, reigns One God, now and forever. AMEN.

These are our prayers. Receive them in your mercy. And grant us, O Lord, your peace—your peace that passes our human understanding. AMEN.

O Lord, your mercy endures forever. Hear the prayers of your people. And grant us the strength and the courage to walk in your ways, all the days of our lives. In the name of Jesus, we pray. AMEN.